Back To Basics
eight sure foundations
for kingdom living

DOUG ROBERTS
BEN PASLEY and TIM F. THORNTON

Find this book online for free on many open source book platforms.
Why? Because we want everyone to read it.

Find it online in every digital format at www.bookshooter.com—*where
the independent author prints ebooks!*

This book was created via a partnership with
www.TheEmpowermentHouse.com—*a coaching service for the author
who wants to be profitably independent.*

Published by Doug Roberts Publishing
Box 321
Frederick, OK 73542

Unless otherwise indicated, all Scripture quotations are from the New
American Standard Bible®, Copyright © 1960, 1962, 1963, 1968, 1971,
1972, 1973, 1975, 1977, 1995 by The Lockman Foundation. Used by
permission." (www.Lockman.org) or the Holy Bible, New
International Version ®. Copyright © 1973, 1978, 1984 International
Bible Society. Used by permission of Zondervan. All rights reserved.
Style modifications to Scripture quotes are author's preference for
emphasis.

Cover Design: Todd Berger
Final Editing: Laurie Thornton, Crucial Book Consulting

Printed in the Unites States of America

ISBN: 978-0-9825992-0-4
Library of Congress Control Number: 2009913100

Dedicated to my children, Amy and Jeremy, and my spiritual sons and daughters. May these foundational truths cause you to stand firm in the grace of the Lord Jesus and grow into full maturity in Him, giving you wisdom to train your own children in the paths of truth so they will be faithful to the Father's plan in their generation.

I also want to say thanks to the fathers that have labored in my life. There is no school on earth that could have taught me more about the Father's love, His kingdom, and how to love the Church. Thank you.

To my wife Rita, without your love, prayers and support I couldn't have made it this far. I so look forward to what the Father has for us to do together in the years to come.

A special thanks to Myra Chinn, Ben Pasley, Tim and Laurie Thornton, and Todd Berger for your labor of love in making this book possible.

Love you all,

Doug Roberts
October 1, 2009

TABLE OF CONTENTS

FOREWORD

It has been said, "First impressions are seldom accurate, but those that are, with the passing of time, grow in stature and substance." This is most certainly true of Doug Roberts. Almost 20 years have passed since I first met "Brother Doug," as he was affectionately called by one of his mentors and my friend, Brother Bob Terrell. I was genuinely impressed by Doug, first as a man and then with his ministry.

Bob Terrell spoke enthusiastically of the prophetic mantle that rested on this son in the faith. It soon became evident to me that Doug exhibited many of the characteristics of a man with a prophetic mantle. He is a person of integrity, and, like most prophets, he is passionate about upholding the name and the nature of *Hashem*. He also has the prophetic disposition of intensity. He is passionate about the Lord's work. And like Amos the prophet, Brother Doug was also a successful farmer. In my office, I have the "miniature bale of genuine Oklahoma cotton" he gave me many years ago.

His ministry has the imprimatur of a prophet. Many of the descriptive terms used in the Hebrew Scriptures are exhibited in his ministry. The first term is *Naba*. The term has a twofold implication. Firstly, it indicates being close to the Lord. In this context Abraham is called such in Genesis 20:7. The word also indicates one who speaks for another as in the case of Aaron who was to be this for Moses in Exodus 7:1. It is evident that Doug has exhibited both intimate proximity to the Lord and a faithfulness in speaking for the Lord over many years.

The second word evidenced in Doug's ministry is the *Chozeh* —one who sees and has insight into the things of the Spirit. This word was frequently translated "seer" as in the case of Samuel in 1 Samuel 9:9.

The third word is *Nataph*, which literally means to drop like dew, but it also indicates abundance—the overflow of the Spirit that comes from deep within.

The fourth word from the Old Testament that is applicable to Doug is *Massah*, which means the "lifter of burdens." People seek out Brother Doug for a word of encouragement, exhortation or comfort. He is, indeed, a lifter of burdens, and a man whose life continues to express these deep, ancient prophetic ministry descriptors throughout his life. One of the things that continues to impress me about Doug is when I have spent time in his presence, even if it was only a short period of time, I have been personally inspired and refreshed. You should expect the same from Doug as you enjoy this, his first book, *Back to Basics*.

Des Evans
November 6, 2009
Senior Pastor, Bethesda Community Church
Fort Worth, Texas

PREFACE

Doug Roberts is one of the wisest men that I know. Of the people I've spent time with who are of great influence in God's kingdom, he is among the least educated by the world's standards. He makes no apologies for this. In fact, he enjoys it immensely. Doug has said some of the most nonsensical things I've ever heard in the English language, but the Lord has used Doug's unapologetic nature, his father's heart, and his deep connection to the Holy Spirit to sharpen me hundreds of times more than He's ever used carefully crafted intellectual arguments or three point sermons with great alliteration and catchy double meanings.

One of Doug's favorite things to say after nonchalantly hitting me with a well-placed challenge or a perfectly timed insight into the Scripture is "...but I'm just from Oklahoma. I don't know as much as you intellectual Colorado people." If you catch him on a particularly good day, he'll start talking about how God chose the foolish to shame the wise, and how his Doug-English is really just freedom in the Spirit to not walk in bondage to the letter of the Law of Webster. This kind of banter is one of the reasons why, before you really know Doug, when you ask him what he's going to teach and he answers, "God's love," it's easy to think he just shrugged you off. You get the feeling that you just asked a weatherman what he was going to talk about and he said "the sky."

This unapologetic attachment to the basics has endeared me to Doug, though. In the recent part of my journey with Jesus, I've found that the most foundational truths are the most life-changing. I can trace most of the hang-ups and dissonances in the way I live out my faith to some belief I entertain that doesn't line up with basic foundational truth. This is especially true of the foundational truth that God really loves me. If we don't believe that one, then we can spend a lot of effort getting nowhere with God.

The heavenly realm of God's love is much bigger than the weather, and is much more worthy of our attention, so let's discover it for ourselves like never before. Let me introduce you to Doug Roberts, who is able to point at the sky as well as anyone I know.

Tim F. Thornton
October 1, 2009

Doug Roberts has been in my life since 1993 when Bob Terrell first introduced me to him. During the early 90's Bob Terrell had such a profound influence on me, especially as it related to understanding the Church and the kingdom of God, that I still refer to him as my spiritual father. Tragically, Bob died in 2000, and when he left he left a sea of men and women in his wake looking around for who might continue the beautiful grace of watching for their souls—pastoring them and caring for their lives. For my wife and I, Doug became that man. No, don't get the idea it was automatic or simple. Doug and his lovely wife, Rita, pursued our hearts and cared for us for years before we could look safely to them as our pastors, or as our spiritual parents, and this was partly due to the deep and lasting impact Brother Bob had on our lives. If these familial terms of endearment make you uncomfortable, I pray you will forgive me for using the only language that adequately expresses our shared love and the function of our relationship together. Doug is a father to me.

In the dedication page of my latest book I made this simple statement which I have really grown to enjoy:

Dedicated to the late Bob Terrel who planted the seed, and to Doug Roberts who now waters.

Thanks, Doug and Rita, for watching for us so well.

The following pages are part narrative, part teaching, and part just the untempered and spontaneous thoughts of three friends. In April of 2009 Doug, Tim, and myself took our old beat up RV into the mountains near our home in Woodland Park, Colorado and for three days did little more than fish, eat, and record our conversations on the kingdom of God. Doug brought his notes on eight basic foundational teachings, and Tim and I brought the food and other distractions. These unabridged recordings can be found at www.timewithdoug.com, and the more orderly, sensical version can be found written on the following pages. Some liberty has been taken to bring theatrical colors and movements to this narrative, but none of these embellishments have strayed more than a few steps from the actual recording.

Take your time; we did.

Ben Pasley
November 15, 2009

1

GOD'S LOVE

Watching the numbered campsite signs through the passenger window, Tim caught a view of the reservoir in the valley below and slowed down to gaze for a moment—it was too far away to see if any fish were rising. He rounded the corner and pulled up next to the old RV which looked as tired as anyone.

"Doug! Ben!" he yelled as he pulled the key from the ignition.

"I thought y'all said it was going to be summer up here," chortled Doug, while Ben handed Tim a plastic cup and poured in the last black coffee from the French press. It was too early for snappy comebacks; Tim sipped his coffee, put it down and started collecting dry twigs fallen from nearby spruce trees.

Minutes later, a fire was blazing and the three were scraping the last scrambled eggs from their paper plates.

"We've got a few things to do around camp, and I'd like to get our first recording going by nine," said Ben as he tossed his plate into the fire, grabbed his keys, and handed Tim some large orange plastic Legos.

"What are these for?" Tim asked.

Doug piled up some of the morning's extra firewood to keep it ready for the next fire as Ben took Tim to the other side of camp and showed him the bubble levels that were built-in to the RV. "These," pointing to the orange blocks in Tim's hand, "are my high tech leveling blocks for the RV."

"Now I know you've left Alabama, Ben, 'cause you're using plastic Lego blocks and not two-by-fours," Doug laughed from around the corner. Ben smiled, fired up the RV, and drove it onto the blocks.

"It's still leaning," Doug yelled to Tim over the sound of the engine, bending down to examine the bubble level.

"Naw, back it up again," yelled Tim up at Ben in the drivers' seat. "One more." He added a block and repositioned them in front of the tire.

"Perfect," said Doug as the RV clumsily halted on top of the blocks for a second time. The engine shut off.

"OK, let's get started." Ben hopped out of the driver's seat. Tim and Doug looked at each other, pleased with their teamwork. The three climbed into the RV's living quarters, partially for shelter from the still-brisk Colorado morning, and partially so the digital audio recorder wouldn't get too much background noise.

Doug shuffled some papers and Ben started to pray out loud as he got his audio recorder set up. Tim and Doug spontaneously joined in. After a few minutes of talking with God, there was a pause.

"You ready to start your book?" asked Ben, "or do you need to take a walk and stir it up?"

"If it's not in me now I don't see how a walk is going to help me any," Doug said with eyes flashing.

Ben touched the record button and squinted for a moment at the recording device to make sure it was on.

Not missing a beat, Doug put his papers aside. "The number one foundation I believe we need in our lives is to understand God's love for us. Most people have a hard time walking in an understanding of who they are in Christ and knowing who God has called them to be. When we're not secure in this foundation, it's hard for us to fulfill our destiny—to walk in what the Father has predestined for us in Christ.

"We simply have to be secure in the Father's love for us.

"In 1974 I came into an understanding of God's love for me. He didn't judge me in the sins that I was in; He loved me in the sins that I was in. God never required a change of me without first giving me a confidence of His love for me. The Bible says it is the kindness of God that leads us to repentance. This is my thirty-fifth year of walking with the Lord and in all those thirty-five years God has always dealt with me out of His love. He has never dealt with me out of His judgment."

Tim thumbed through his Bible. "So God's kindness, not His judgment," he repeated, has truly led to repentance?"

"A lot of people imagine that God is just waiting for them to mess up so He can judge them, rebuke them, and chasten them. That is so contrary to the heart of the Father. God has a plan for us. The Bible talks about how God has predestined before the beginning of time good works for us to do in Christ Jesus. If we are not secure in the Father's love for us, then it is going to be hard to fulfill the destiny He has given us in His son, Jesus, because we will always worry about whether we are going to be a disappointment to Him.

"Now, we will talk more about this in the chapter on suffering, but it's important to mention here, too. Every time you go through a difficult time, no matter what it is—tribulation, persecution, or whatever—the devil always challenges you with 'If God really loved you, these things would not be happening to you.' The devil will always challenge the love of the Father concerning you.

"So I'll say it again," Doug emphasized. "The number one foundation that we have to have in our lives is knowing God loves us."

Ben nodded and smiled, "It's as if the devil were saying, 'You wouldn't be suffering—you wouldn't be uncomfortable—if God really loved you.'"

Doug answered, "Yet if I understand God's love for me, then I understand that the things that I am going through will work for my good. Romans says, 'All things work together for good to those who love God and are called according to His purpose.' When I understand that truth then I can come out of my temporal mindset that wonders why hard things happen, and I can come into my eternal mindset that knows that the situation is working to help me be able to do what God has called me to do. If I guard my heart and rule my soul, that will keep me from allowing the devil to battle in my mind about who I am as a son in the Father's love.

"John 3:16 says, 'God so loved the world that He gave His only begotten son that whosoever shall believe in Him should not perish but have eternal life.' God loved the earth, and so we can realize that God created it as a place for His kingdom to be established, where His sons could fulfill their destiny in His kingdom. The kingdom of God is an unshakable kingdom.

"The devil knows that if he can keep us questioning our identity and the sonship that God has for us, we will never fulfill that destiny that God has predestined for us. So the devil will always try to keep us in a temporal mindset that asks 'why is this happening?' or 'why am I having to do this?' We need to quit asking the question 'why' and just embrace the momentary and light afflictions we're in so that we don't lose focus of the eternal purpose God has for us. That eternal purpose is to be sons of the Most High executing righteous judgments here on earth. We are to manifest His kingdom in all that we do.

"'Jesus, establish my kingdom,' is what we often hear from one another, but it is not God's plan to establish *your* kingdom. His plan is to establish *His* kingdom.

"In most people's religious systems we often hear teachings about how to redeem fallen man. However, Jesus has already redeemed the fallen man. His work is not just to bring man back up to the plateau of where he was before he fell into sin, but to the high place where God created him to be. It is bringing man into the fullness of what God has called him to be in Christ Jesus."

Deep in thought, Ben looked around and then said with a half-smile, "When I think about my history growing up, I remember spending 90% of our time talking about how to get redeemed, how to get saved, how to get fixed, how to get restored to righteousness, and how to get over feelings of guilt. This was like the entirety of the work of Jesus. But you are saying it is only the doorway to where we are supposed to be heading?"

"If we understand the foundation of God's love for us then salvation is not the question," Doug continued. "In Luke it talks about Adam as the son of God. So God created the earth and put His son, Adam, on it to rule that which He had annexed to be

His kingdom. Then sin appeared, so Jesus came to make an atonement for sin. God's original intent was not just to bring salvation to us in Jesus. God's original intent was to have His kingdom established on the earth and that we would fulfill our destiny as sons on the earth.

"It is interesting that after Adam sinned he noticed that he was naked. God asked Adam 'who told you that you are naked?' God had clothed Adam in flesh because he was a spirit man first. So now we are clothed in Christ, because we are spirit men."

Tim looked up from his notebook, grasping the thought. "That had not occurred to me. So you mean that in God's eyes Adam was not naked, because God had given him a body of flesh as his clothing? What an interesting thought—what we can be so concerned with trying to correct is not even really a problem for God."

"The devil has us all off track in trying not to loose our salvation," said Doug. "Salvation is a done deal. I am saved. I am being saved. I will be saved. That's important but it doesn't have anything to do with my understanding of who I am in the foundation of God's love for me.

"Sin is really not an issue because sin has already been dealt with in Christ," Doug smiled and laughed as he often does on the points he enjoys the most. "The Scripture says that those that are in Christ have ceased from sin. Sin is not something we always have to battle. If you don't understand God's love for you, then you are always trying to get back to the plateau of being sinless. Most people spend their whole life's energy trying to overcome sin instead of recognizing that sin has already been overcome, and all we have to do is to fulfill our destiny in the true identity of who we are in Christ. We do this only in an understanding of God's love.

"Ephesians says to 'watch what God does and then do it. Children learn proper behavior from their parents.' Well, mostly what God does is just love you." He continued reading, "'Keep company with Him and learn a life of love. Observe how Christ loved us. His love is not cautious but extravagant. He did not love us in order to get something from us but to give everything of Himself to us.' Most people can't come into an understanding of the extravagant love of the Father because they are still trying to earn God's love."

"We spend most of our time talking about sin as if it were some sort of legal contract, a set of rules, or a formula," added Ben, leaning forward and subtly shaking his head. "But those ideas are all really secondary to what we are talking about here. If you spend your whole life trying to define salvation by categories, teaching of laws, rules, contracts or formulas, that's wrong."

"On their own, those things miss the point," Tim jumped in, now truly beginning to shake off the morning's cold. "They might be true, but there's a difference between talking about how and why we are saved and just being saved!"

"God's love just covers it completely so we don't have to hack it into a million intellectual arguments," said Ben, relaxing into his chair.

Doug continued. "If you look at I John, it says, 'This is love not that we loved God but that He loved us and He sent His son to us as payment for our sins.' It's not that I love God but that He loves me. God was secure in His love for me before I ever responded to His love. God's love for me does not depend on what I do or how I act.

"Now when I was in the ways of the world, doing the sins I did and not knowing Jesus, God loved me. When I got saved and repented of my sins and began walking as a son, God loved me.

God does not love me more now than He loved me then. God loved me the same when I was a sinner as He loves me now that I'm a son. His love is no greater or no less. I cannot earn God's love and I cannot lose God's love. What is affected is my relationship with Him. When I was in the world as a sinner, I did not have a relationship with the Father so I couldn't respond and really know His love. Once I became a believer, my relationship with Him changed so now I can respond to His love and know His love. His love for me is the same. His love does not depend on what I do or don't do."

"It is amazing how often we intellectually grasp a principle like this and might even preach and teach it, but still discover places in our lives where we act like we don't have a clue about it. I've had times when I could talk and teach and write about grace all day, and then be full of striving and not at rest in my own soul," Tim admitted.

"This is what religion tries to do," said Doug, "it puts us in a mindset of performance, that I have to earn God's love by keeping this, doing this, and by not doing this or doing that. But when we understand God's love, we know that it is not what we have done that saves us; it is what He did through His son, Jesus. Who can earn salvation? What can you pay for the cost of your sins? Jesus paid the price. He paid it on my behalf. It was God's choice to give His son to redeem me from that which I was."

Ben took off his glasses, as if relaxing into the truth Doug was speaking, thought a minute, and then asked, "How do you respond to those who say, 'No Doug, God did everything but now we have to respond and do something, too. Don't we have to be the ones to have faith?'"

"Have faith in what?" Doug's response was unexpected by his companions. The loud question rang through the RV, and Tim and Ben smiled at Doug's boldness. He continued, "Faith in what you can do, or faith in what He has done? If you have faith in what God has done then you settle the issue that He is God. And because He is God you can't add to it or take away from it.

"Isaiah 46 says, 'I am God and there is no one like me. I declare the end before the beginning.' Now, I believe we can choose to walk away from God's plan. But I believe if our heart is to walk in the purpose of what the Father has for us, then no weapon formed against me is going to prosper. It says that nothing can pluck me out of the hand of the Father. I can walk away from the relationship I experience with the Father, but I don't believe that the Father will walk away from me."

Ben continued the thought: "People talk about their faith as though it is some sort of machine. Hollywood stars and rock stars talk about their faith. Christians say, 'because I have faith I am saved.' People settle on that as though faith were some sort of a magic word. As if in and of itself it had some sort of a quality or purpose in it. But we have to question like you did, Doug, and say, 'Faith in what?' That is amazing."

"We are saved by grace through faith," Tim added. "Faith is not the source of our salvation. It is just the vehicle."

Doug nodded, "Faith is a gift that is given to us by our Father because He loves us. God gave His Son because He loves the world. God gave us Jesus. He gave us faith. He gave us the Holy Spirit. If you walk in the love that He has given us in Christ, if you walk in the faith that He has given us, and if you walk in the Holy Spirit that He has given us, you will fulfill your destiny and understand the purpose He has called you to.

"The Bible talks about truth and grace in Christ Jesus. I believe that the Holy Spirit brings revelation of truth. But without the platform of God's grace, it is hard to walk in the truth. A lot of times we try to walk in a revelation of truth outside of God's grace, so then we make a tradition or a law out of it and then it makes the word of God 'of none effect.'" Doug reflected to Tim and Ben, as he rifled through his notes, that "*none effect*" was a quote from King James and that the verse could be found in the first part of Matthew 15.

"Sometimes I have seen folks that may have a prophetic gift or received a prophetic word, and the word was true," said Ben. "They even say that they saw a Scripture that gave them a command to do something, but because they weren't sure of God's love for them, they turned that truth into another new thing to strive in. They sort of perverted the whole thing and it all went sour. The thing in and of itself was true; the revelation was true but they didn't have confidence in God's love, so they could not enjoy the truth."

"They didn't understand the grace to apply the truth," explained Doug. "It was according to works, not according to grace. I think you can take that same principle in John where Jesus says, 'You search the Scripture because you think in them you are going to find eternal life but you are unwilling to come to Me.' The Scripture is the foundation of truth that we walk in, but if you just know the Scripture without the love of the Father, it is just knowledge.

"There is a Scripture in Ephesians 3 that says, 'To know the love of Christ which surpasses knowledge, that you may be filled up to all the fullness of God.' How do you obtain the fullness of God? Through knowing the love of Christ, and that is more than knowledge—it surpasses it!

"What is the *love of Christ that surpasses knowledge*? It is the foundation of having your confidence in knowing who you are in Christ Jesus. Your identity is not in yourself. It is in Christ, and you are secure in the love of the Father as Jesus is. It is not really the things that you do or don't do; you just walk in the finished work of Christ."

Tim put down his notebook, reflecting, "What freedom!" He looked out the window and breathed deeply, as if taking time to soak it all in.

But Doug wasn't ready to stop there. "The Scripture talks about how God is love. God is not a God of love. He is love.

"In different religions you might have the different statues, like Buddha and the god of this and the god of that. But as I said, our God is not a God of love. He is love. There is a difference. I am not that familiar with all the religions in the world but I'm sure there is a god of love, like there is a god of the moon, a god of the sun, and all of that. But if we just try to categorize God as a God of love outside of knowing that He *is* love then we miss the fullness of who He is."

Tim agreed, "So love is not a value outside of God by which He is measured. He defines what love is!"

"I believe that if you do not have the number one foundation that God loves you, then you are always battling the issues of what you have to do," continued Doug. "When you just settle in and rest in knowing that God loves you, no matter what happens in your life—good or bad—you know it is working for the good. The Scripture says, "All things work together for the good.' Why can we rest in that? Because we know that God loves us. God is not chastening us to kill us; He is chastening us to conform us to His image. Why does He want us to be conformed to His image? Because we have to execute righteousness on the earth to establish His kingdom. So He is conforming us to the love that He is so that we will be loving ambassadors on the earth to represent Him."

Ben looked at Doug and then at Tim. "I have made a mistake on more than one occasion in talking about sonship," he ventured. "Because sonship is our destiny, and the Father loves us as sons and calls us into His family, you would think that would be a great place to start. But sometimes I say the word *sonship,* and then I find out that people aren't sure that God loves them. The result is that they just freak out because they feel like sonship is just another thing to work for and they are not there yet. They are not sure if they have done enough to avoid rejection by the Father. So if you don't understand God's love, then you can't even come into sonship. It wouldn't even make any sense to you."

Doug replied, "I have a son. He is thirty-two years old. He was born my son and will always be my son. As we grow in our relationship and as he experiences my love he is not only my son, but he is also my friend. If you take that principle then when you are grounded in God's love and you know that God loves you as a son, then you can come into a place of friendship with Him. In John 15 it says, 'No longer do I call you slaves, for the slave does not know what his master is doing; but I have called you friends, for all things that I have heard from My Father I have made known to you.'

"You can have a son's understanding but still walk mostly in a slave mentality, with slave instincts," Doug explained. "But when you have a son's intimate, instinctual knowledge of the Father's love, then you walk as a friend in your sonship with the Father and you know the Father's heart. You know the Father's heart because you spend time with Him and you walk with Him in relationship and in fellowship."

"You could know, factually, that you are God's son. You could understand that from Scripture, but you can act like a slave and have slave instincts still ruling in you," Ben re-worded Doug's assertion as if laying out the distinction in his own mind. "The parable of the prodigal son is a perfect example. The older brother's inheritance was his to claim any time he wanted it, but he felt like it wasn't his. He did not understand his identity as a son so he had never even asked his father for his inheritance…as if he didn't know he had one. He didn't really know the love of the father. It's like he said, 'well, I have done everything that you have told me to do. I have performed for you. I have danced for you. I have played in the band for you. Why did you show so much favor to my brother who just went crazy and blew his inheritance?' His whole identity was in what he did to please the father and he never really knew the father's heart even though he was around him all the time. It's not that he argued and said, 'I am not your son.' That was not his argument. It was, 'I don't think you love me enough. I'm going to have to strive and contend to try and earn what is mine.'"

Doug jumped into the parable without hesitation, "And what happened when the brother went away, squandered his inheritance, and then came back? What was there? The love of his father was there. The love of the Father had even more inheritance for him than what he had squandered."

Tim pointed out another dimension of the story: "Even though the prodigal came back with a slave mentality as well, saying 'I want to be a servant in my father's house,' and thinking maybe he could earn his way back in by performing good enough to live on the outskirts, just under the shelter, and that would be enough. He had the same attitude, really, that the brother who stayed at home had, but the father's reaction was totally different than what they both expected. The father's love didn't give the son a chance to earn it, because the father was waiting and looking for his son to return. That is a true picture of the Father's mercy, not giving us what we deserve, but inviting us to walk in the fullness of the grace given us, just because of his love."

Ben laughed, "The father totally kung-fu'd that idea all together. He blew up that earning-equation."

Doug was still in the midst of the parable. "What did the father do? The first thing he did was ask for the best robe so he could put it on his son. Symbolically, what was the best robe the Father had to clothe the lost son with?" Doug paused for effect. "It was *Christ*. So the father said 'bring out Christ to cover my lost son.' So we are clothed in Christ!"

He continued, "Then he said to bring out the ring. He put the ring on his newly returned son. The ring is a symbol of the father's authority. Imagine the ring with the father's seal on it, so that anything the son seals with it is a debt the father is taking care of. Then the father said to bring out the sandals. What do the sandals represent?" Doug asked rhetorically. "The sandals are a prophetic picture of our walk to go establish the kingdom with the revelation of what God has given us. So here we are: clothed in Christ, walking with the authority of the Father, with a prophetic understanding to establish the Father's kingdom, covered with the mantle that He gave us in Christ."

Ben lifted up his feet. "With Dad's sandals on, you could be a son no matter where you went. The prodigal didn't act like a son when he was in another country squandering his inheritance. He acted like something else. But now that he had the sandals on, I think they would represent that he could walk anywhere and still be comfortable in the love of the father and know that he was a son. He was establishing and walking in the authority of the father's kingdom."

"Yes," said Doug. "But there's more. Then the father said to bring out the fattened calf. The fattened calf is what?"

Now Doug was really enjoying this cascading line of rhetorical questions and couldn't wait to answer his own question: "The fatted calf represents the Father's provision!"

Now he was on a roll. "When we are walking in the mantle of the Father's love, when we are walking in the authority of the Father, when we are walking in the prophetic anointing to establish His kingdom, then there is abundance in all that we do," he said. "The fattened calf speaks of the abundance of the loving father. He didn't say bring out a chicken or a pig. He said bring out the fattened calf, which is about abundance and celebration. In fact, the parable even says that then there was celebration. Celebration happens when you are walking in the love of the Father, in the authority of the Father, and the prophetic advancement of His kingdom with the abundance of what He has. Then the joy of the Lord is being established because righteousness reigns.

"When righteousness reigns there is peace. There is righteousness, peace, and joy in the Holy Spirit."

"You mean the results of the expressions of the kingdom are these things: righteousness, peace and joy?" Ben asked, more for emphasis than clarification.

Doug paused, realizing he'd been deeply engrossed in the parable. "Yes," he said, then smiled, returning in his mind to the RV, where the morning sun was now streaming full-force through the windows and warming things nicely.

He glanced again at his notes and continued, "In order to have an understanding of the love of the Father, we first have to know that the Father loves us and His love was not found in our choosing Him, but in Him choosing us. There again the Bible talks about how God chose you and appointed you that you would go and bear fruit. If we are grounded in the Father's love then it is not about what I do but it is about what he did. I do what I do because He did what He did. If He didn't do what He did then I couldn't do what I do.

"He chose me and he appointed me. To do what? *To go and bear fruit.* You remember the blessings that we talked about the prodigal son having received when he returned to the Father. In the same way, the Father chose me, the Father gives me authority, and the Father gives me provision. Therefore I don't worry about what tomorrow holds because the Father's grace for me is for today. The enemy tries to come in and rob me of my joy today because of my fear of tomorrow. That is why it says 'take every thought captive'.

"The whole foundation of knowing the Father's love for us settles the issue of worrying for the rest of our lives. It says that God knew the end before the beginning. He has predestined us before the beginning of time. If you want to really stretch that, I believe that the Father had a plan for us to fulfill in Christ. So He spoke the world into existence so that He could annex it to establish His kingdom, that we could fulfill our destiny. So if I am secure in that, then I'm sitting here knowing that God made this world just for me to fulfill my destiny because He loves me that much. If God went to that much trouble to speak the world into existence and to establish all the things that we see just for me to fulfill my destiny, then how can I worry and question and doubt His love for me?"

Tim looked up from something he was drawing in his notebook. "You keep talking about eternal purpose and our destiny," he said. "You said that we are not just saved, as if eternity was the afterthought in the story of sin. Instead, sin is a sidebar in the story of eternity. Understanding that, we must actually be saved to something—getting saved is not the end. We are saved to our eternal purpose and destiny—to our place as sons. Can you talk more about what we're saved to and what you mean when you talk about our eternal purpose and destiny?"

"Well, eternal purpose is different in each one of us," Doug obliged. "The grace that God has given me is different than that grace that God has given you. That's why we don't compare ourselves with one another—that is not a wise thing to do.

"In Christ we have been made perfect. My eternal purpose that God has called me to might be completely different than what your eternal purpose is. And the differences and similarities are all because of the grace given to us, the measure of who we are, the makeup and the DNA that we have.

"God didn't make clones. If all three of us were just alike in everything that we do, then two of us would not be needed. We need each other. We need to walk in relationship and in family with one another. We need to walk in the light because there is an inheritance stored up in the saints. So there's inheritance in the eternal purpose God has called me to walk in, and you can tap into it. There is an inheritance in you—your eternal purpose that God has called you to walk in—that I can tap into. The devil does not want us to tap into one another through relationship and family because he knows when we do, the kingdom is going to be established."

"Tim asked a question about eternal destiny and I noticed you are defining it now as something that we are living in presently," ventured Ben. "It is not all a future package that you get to pop open in the next era. How great to think that a part of your destiny as a son is that you get to act like who you are now and enjoy other people instead of waiting for glory."

"Yes," Tim agreed. "'Your will be done on earth as it is in heaven.' As we work out our salvation we are restored to live in that eternal story—the one that began before sin and will go on after sin—right now instead of later. And you're saying the eternal story has a lot to do with being together, being able to 'tap into' one another."

Doug replied, "The ultimate goal of God is not just to get me to heaven. We are already seated with Christ. If God's ultimate goal, His eternal purpose for me, was heaven, then as soon as I got saved, He would have just taken me and I would be in heaven. But it says that 'God so loved the earth that He gave His only Son.'

"So evidently there is something about the earth that God loves and wants to establish here. If God just wanted me to be in heaven, then when I accepted Jesus—there is no other way to the Father except though the Son—I would've instantly been in heaven.

"What does religion tell us? Religion tells us that God's ultimate intent is to get us saved so we can move in to our mansion in heaven, but the truth is, God wants us to establish His kingdom here on earth. John 14 says that 'in my Father's house are many dwelling places.' The word 'place' here means an abiding or indwelling of God in us. The passage goes on to say, "if it was not so, I would have told you, for I go to prepare a place for you.' The word 'place' there is like a region or a city or area, which refers to our rule in His kingdom on the earth. According to the religious mindset, we will always be hoping we do not mess up and lose our salvation and that sin doesn't rule over us, because we just have to hold on until we get to heaven. Well, in that case, the devil and religion have robbed us of our freedom in Christ. Where the Spirit of the Lord is, though, there is freedom, liberty, peace, and all that good stuff. Heaven is not my goal. Being obedient today and walking in my destiny are my goals, for this is the day that the Lord has called me to walk in faith.

"I have to ask myself, 'what has God called me to do today?' I don't worry about what He calls me to do tomorrow. I want to fulfill His purpose today. I'm His son today and I have grace today."

Tim nodded, subconsciously tapping his pen on his notebook. "In contrast but not in conflict with that, I often feel a longing for rightness that has not fully come upon us in our present world," he said. "And yet the Scripture does not say that creation is longing and groaning for us all to get done with this place and go to heaven. It says that it is groaning and waiting for the sons of God to be revealed."

Ben agreed. "I feel like sometimes when I meditate or when I am walking through the forest or in the mall that the earth sighs relief when I show up. It feels like there's something about the atmosphere. I think the sons of God are the most environmentally friendly things in the world. When we walk into an environment, we make it better. And the earth says, 'Thank you for being here, son of God. I have been waiting for you to show up and just be here because now I feel like I am purposeful and it is not a waste that I am a tree out here in the middle of the woods for nothing.'

"I believe that wherever we set our feet, that the kingdom of God is established," proclaimed Doug calmly. "God said in Genesis that He gave man dominion over everything on the earth. However, how many things on the earth have dominion over us instead! We are here on the earth to rule and reign in righteousness. Not to just maintain the environment for the sake of itself."

Tim smirked, "We act like we are not supposed to be here."

"I plant trees because I love trees," explained Doug. "I like trees in my yard. I live in Oklahoma and we don't have any trees unless you plant them. I don't plant trees just for the sake of the environment. I plant trees for my sake because it gives me pleasure."

"The reason you don't trust a man to dominate the earth is because you don't trust the heart of a man," Ben's tone was contemplative. "I can trust you, Tim, because you have the heart of the Father. I can trust you, too, Doug. If I trust your heart, then I can trust you to take care of things. That is how I see our dominion over the world. I do not see it as some have falsely assumed, that dominion *equals* exploitation. No. For sons, dominion equals taking care of our home."

"You could take that concept into the practical everyday things," Doug added. "I have a home that my wife and I live in. We have raised our children in it. When I come into my home, I don't destroy my home. My home is a place that I can rest in. If God has given us the earth to be our home in which we'll establish His kingdom, then naturally we are going to maintain and take care of our home. But our identity and value is not in our home. Our identity is in the love of the Father.

"If you ask people why Jesus came to the earth, one answer would be 'to destroy the works of the devil.' That is true. Jesus did come to destroy the works of the devil. But He also came to reestablish the kingdom of God on earth that Adam lost. He also came to bring many sons unto glory. He also came to fulfill the destiny of the Father's predetermined plan on the earth: that His sons would rule the earth and establish His kingdom in it. That was the idea when He made Adam and breathed into him the breath of life, so he could rule and have dominion on the earth.

"Somewhere along the line, because we hadn't understood the full love of the Father and the foundational principles of what the initial purposes of the Father's heart were, we slipped into a salvation mentality where we think the goal is just to redeem men from their sin and hold on until we get to heaven.

"We have missed 99% of what the Father's heart is," Doug said, with a slight tone of disappointment. "That is because we don't know the heart of the Father because we are not secure in His love for us. Once we become secure in His love then we begin to see how great a love the Father has bestowed upon us that we are called His children."

Tim sat up straight. "I see an echo here of what we talked about with slaves not knowing the Father's business or His heart, but His friends know His heart. A slave doesn't know the purposes and goals of the master; he just thinks about doing a good enough job to keep his place under the roof. But when we're God's friends—His family—we don't just think about what we can do or not do to stay inside His favor, we think about what His heart is, what His dreams and goals are, and what He delights in. It's a question of making up our minds about who we are to God. Are we His slaves or are we going to agree with what He's spoken and be His family?"

Doug smiled through his words, "Ben wrote this song that says, 'Why don't we go with He loves me?' If I'm in doubt, I don't really have a better choice than to go ahead and believe that He loves me. If anything is true, it is that God loves us. I believe that I am God's favorite son but I also believe that you can be His favorite son, too. I really believe that. What keeps you from believing that you are God's favorite son? Your mind—when you choose to believe the things that you see versus the things that are eternal."

"On that subject," Tim said, "I would like for you to talk about how we are to deal with the things that we do see or that happen to us that don't line up in our minds with how we understand God's eternal purpose and kingdom. I have heard you say that if you have the foundation that God loves you in all things then you can accept suffering and you can accept joy and abundant provision, both from the same God. That is because you know that everything He does is because He is love and it comes from love. On a practical level, I think people would really like to have a good understanding of how we are to think of sufferings like sickness, war, and other terrible situations. Are we to say, 'Well, this is the lot in life that the Father has given me and I just have to accept that suffering is coming from His hand?' On the other hand, there are times when something in us says, 'Jesus, bring Your kingdom. This is not the way things are supposed to be.' How do you decide?"

"Well, I want to talk about that more when we get to the chapter on rejoicing in suffering, but I will say that in my own life," answered Doug, "I farmed for twenty-five years. There was one particular season that I planted wheat and my wheat got hailed out right before I got ready to harvest it. Then, my cattle started dropping dead of lead poisoning right before I started to sell them. Then after that my cotton got hailed out too! And I said, 'God, what is going on?' And God said, 'I just wanted to show you what you could do.'

"I had made a statement prior to that year that I could restore what I had lost 'because I am a good farmer and rancher.' Sometimes God doesn't cause the circumstances, but He allows circumstances to take place just to show us what we can do.

"In Jeremiah 17 God said, 'Cursed is the one who trusts in man, who depends on flesh for his strength and whose heart turns away from the Lord…he will not see prosperity when it comes.'

"The prosperity of the Lord is always around us. Yes, I can trust in my own ability. I can trust in my own flesh. I can trust in my own gifting and my own strengths. Some of them might even be what God has given me. But when I trust in them, I am not able to see the provision of the Lord and who I am and what God has called me to do."

Doug continued quoting Jeremiah like he was talking to an old friend. "But 'blessed is the man who trusts in the Lord and whose trust is the Lord. For he will be like a tree planted by the water, that extends its roots by a stream and will not fear when the heat comes; but its leaves will be green, and it will not be anxious in a year of drought nor cease to yield fruit.'

"See, God had to deal with me in an area in which I wouldn't trust Him. I had to learn to allow the Lord to be my trust. It comes back to understanding the foundation of God's love for me. If I'm not secure in God's love for me, then I can't allow the Father to be my trust. I can trust in Him on the surface, but I still have to perform because somewhere inside I think He is not really going to take care of me. After my cattle dropped dead, my wheat got hailed out, and my cotton got hailed out, and God told me He wanted to show me what I could do in my own strength, I asked 'why couldn't you have just told me that instead of letting me experience it?'"

Tim and Ben laughed and looked expectantly, waiting for the answer.

"Well, I am kind of hardheaded," Doug explained, realizing the question was not rhetorical for his friends. "Sometimes you can tell me something but I really don't get it. But if I experience it, then I got it.

"The next year, I planted cotton and the boll weevils were devouring my crop, so I was out speaking to the boll weevils in my cotton and rebuking them in Jesus' name.

"I got laughed at by some other folks who said, 'we're *sprayin'* and Doug's *prayin'*,' but I had some of the best dry land cotton in Tillman County that year because my trust wasn't in my ability to farm, but in God. My trust was in God's ability to work through me for what He called me to do. I think a lot of times God allows situations to happen to really settle issues within us that He is the King and it is not really about what I do, it is about who He is."

Tim nodded, satisfied. He knew he'd get more than he bargained for when he asked Doug about those sorts of things.

"The Bible says that in the last days there will be wars," said Doug. "Now, ultimately, President Bush didn't start any wars. God didn't start any wars. We are simply going to have wars in this world. We are going to have earthquakes. We are going to have tornadoes. The Bible says we are going to have them. That does not affect God's ability to be love or to be the King of Kings.

"Many people ask, 'if God is the God of love then why are these things happening?'

"Some of these things might be happening because of the choices that man has made. In my opinion, when I sin or do something contrary to what God says, then I come out of God's provision to take care of the situation. That is because I'm trusting in the strength of my arm. I am saying, 'God I don't need you in this deal. I can take care of this.' If that is where I am at in my heart then why should I think God is obligated to do anything for me? I have said I can do it myself.

"I think a lot of things happen because we choose to come out of the government of who the Father is and into our own government, trying to be the king of our own little world.

"I know what I can produce, and that is death." Doug paused, then added, "We want God to do His part. But then we blame God for not doing His part when we have not done our part. It goes back to understanding the love of the Father."

"And raising our vision to see the whole story," Tim added.

"Yep," said Doug. "I am settled that God knows my end before my beginning. Sometime in the 70's I said, 'God, I'm tired of trying to walk in your purpose and your perfect will. You know my heart, so everything I do, I'm going to believe that is your perfect will. If it is not your perfect will, then let me know.

"There are days I will just go along and play golf and go hunting and do whatever and God blesses it. There are other days where God will say, 'What are you getting ready to do?'

"I answer and He says, 'That is not my perfect will for you today.'

"Then He speaks to me what I need to do. I don't sit around wondering what God's perfect will is for me. I just believe that everything I do is God's perfect will for me until He corrects me and says it's not."

"'It's God who works in you to will and act according to His good purpose,'" remarked Tim.

"I have faith in God being God," said Doug. "I believe God even likes being God, so I definitely don't have to be God for Him."

"Do you think that's what the heart of a son is really like?" asked Ben. "Is that what this is really about? I don't know many people that walk in the confidence that being themselves is God's will in their life. Do you think that's how it works?"

"It is the simplicity of the gospel once you are secure in the Father's love," answered Doug with a poet's tone.

There was a moment of bright silence, then Doug got his rancher voice back. "I have a young grandson, and he will be on the bed and he will just say, 'Paw-Paw catch me.' Then he will just jump, knowing that I will catch him. Now there are times I almost hurt myself trying to catch him because I didn't know he was going to jump, but I knew I had to catch him because I didn't want to put doubt in his understanding of his grandfather's love.

"Jesus, when He was baptized by John, came out of the water, and they heard a voice: 'This is my Son in whom I am well pleased.' Right after that He was led to the wilderness by the Spirit for forty days to be tempted by the devil and to fast. That doesn't seem fair. The people heard, 'This is my son in whom I am well pleased.' Then He had to go to wilderness for forty days to be tempted by the devil and to not get anything to eat.

"If I had been Jesus, I might have said 'Don't you realize I am your Son? Didn't you hear what you just said? Now you are sending me to the desert to be tempted? What is that about?'

"The first thing that happened in the desert when the devil came was that he questioned the word that God has spoken to Jesus. The devil asked Him, 'if you are God's Son, then turn these rocks into bread.'

"Jesus was secure in the love of the Father and He knew who He was as God's Son so He didn't respond to the devil in performance. He just responded with what the Father had said.

"A lot of times we get into traps because we don't know who we are in Christ and we are not confident in the love of the Father so when the devil comes and questions what the Father has said about us, we try to perform for the devil."

Doug's tone became even more frank as he continued: "What happens when you perform for the devil? You put the devil in the position of being the judge. Jesus could have turned those stones into bread. But if He had turned them into rye bread then the devil would have said, 'If you were really the Son of God then you would have turned them into wheat bread.'

"Jesus didn't put the devil into a position of being His judge by performing for him. He responded with a confidence of what the Father had spoken."

Ben observed, "He knew who He was."

"What a powerful thing that is," Tim added. "When we're secure in who we are, which comes from knowing the complete love with which the Father sees us and agreeing with what He's spoken, we don't have to be filled with self-doubt and criticism all the time. We, in Christ, know who we are.

"What we can produce in the flesh is death, but when we have been robed in Christ, we do His will," Tim continued with not a little wonder in his voice. "You don't see the prodigal son wearing his father's robe going back into the father's bedroom to consult the rule book all the time to see what he should be doing. If you are wearing Christ, you should be expecting to do God's perfect will, just as Christ does."

Tim continued connecting the dots. "Once we know the heart of Christ we have a new heart. I think we should be expecting to reflect Christ and express Christ to the world. I do think it's a fair expectation. Then if the Holy Spirit says, 'What are you doing? I have something else for you,' then that is the way the He leads us.

"When we understand who we are in Christ then we could be doing God's perfect will without even having to think about it or look at what the rules are." It was clear in Tim's eyes that he was already celebrating that truth, but he shrugged his shoulders at Ben and Doug, waiting for confirmation.

"Yes!" said Doug. "It is no longer I who lives but Christ in me. It is in Him that I live and move and have my being. And what I do, it is no longer I but it is Christ in me working through me to accomplish His purpose for me. That is being secure in the love of the Father, clothed in the fullness of God's grace for me in Christ. We just need to rest in knowing that God is for us, that He deeply loves us, and that He knows the plans He has for us."

WALKING IN FORGIVENESS

The sun was bright and strong, warming the huge boulders and scrubby trees on the other side of the lake by the time Doug, Ben, and Tim found their way through the woods, down a steep slope, and finally to the shore. They set up their fishing gear and chatted about how beautiful the scenery was, what the depth of the reservoir must be, and how good it felt to be out despite the 9,000 feet of altitude presenting particular challenges to Doug's Oklahoma lungs during the descent from camp. Nearby, a man wearing oddly inappropriate hip-hop garb was teaching his three-year-old daughter to fish.

Ben reeled in a nice-sized rainbow trout on his second cast and had no trouble bragging about it. Tim, accustomed exclusively to fly-fishing, avoided giving Ben any encouragement for catching a fish on a bait-casting rig. Fly-fishermen are a prejudiced bunch. Tim stood off a few paces trying not to call attention to his awkward wielding of the spin-casting setup and the fact that his fingers were bleeding from wrestling the mass of treble hooks protruding from his little plastic lure. The fish-like plastic lure was not submitting to his authority.

Finally getting things in order, Tim pressed his thumb on the reel and flung his lure toward the water.

Kerplunk. Splash.

Two splashes? Was a monster fish taking the lure already? Ben, already reeling in another fish, gave a look of surprise followed by a high-pitched laugh that echoed off the rocks on the other side of the reservoir when he saw Tim, puzzled, holding a two foot long section of rod from which a tangle of fishing line extended about ten feet into the lake and disappeared.

Doug observed (without any effort to hide his delight) that Tim's thumb was still holding the reel's button down, but that the rest of the reel had joined the lure out in the lake—along with the entire tip-half of the rod! During Tim's mighty cast he had pushed the reel's guts completely out of the housing with his thumb and, as it shot out toward the lake, it had grabbed the end of the rod and took it all—hook, line, and sinker as it were—right out into the lake.

Tim sighed, mustered up a laugh at the absurdity of the situation, and sat down to draw the tangles and pieces of reel and lure from the place where they'd settled on the bottom of the lake.

Afternoon clouds were gathering when, after long minutes of untangling, cutting, and re-tying, the fishing rod was back to its original state.

"Welp, ready to go do the chapter on forgiveness?" asked Doug, slyly smiling at Tim's near total absence of any angling whatsoever.

"Yeah."

Back in the RV, Ben had already turned on the voice recorder
when the four-minute timer chimed, telling the men it was time
to plunge the coffee press. Doug started in on the conversation as
Ben poured the coffee: "The second most important foundation
that a Christian needs in his or her life," he said, "is the ability to
walk in forgiveness. I believe there is something about forgiveness
that most Christians are not aware of—we don't understand the
sowing and reaping process of it.

"For me, the first principle is to know that your sins are
forgiven by the Father. The second is that we have to forgive
ourselves. A lot of people don't have a problem realizing that the
Father has forgiven their sins, but they have a problem forgiving
themselves of their sins. After we have those two things resolved,
we can get to the third principle, forgive others.

"Let's start with this third principle, forgiving others. Let's
look at some Scriptures that talk about not being ignorant about
the plan of the enemy that ensnares us because of our
unforgiveness and the judgments that we make. There is a
principle in the New Testament that we see in three different
places where Jesus tells his disciples that if we don't forgive, our
Heavenly Father will not forgive us.

"Matthew 18, Mark 11, and Matthew 6 all say that if you
don't forgive, your Heavenly Father will not forgive you.
Unforgiveness, according to Matthew 18, as I see the Scripture, is
the only thing that can reinstate a person's debt.

"Look at this parable in Matthew 18: The king said to his
slave, 'pay me what you owe me.' The slave said, 'I can't pay you,'"
Doug paraphrased the story in his usual plainly spoken way
which always seemed to belie the fact that he was describing
eternal truths and spiritual principles. "Then the king said, 'Well,
I am going to throw you in prison till you pay all that you owe

me.' The slave pleaded with him and said, 'Have mercy on me and I will repay you all that I owe you.' Then the king forgave him all his debt.

"Then that same slave went out and found another slave that owed him, but the slave whose debt the King canceled didn't forgive the one who owed him. Instead of forgiving like the King had forgiven him, he threw the one who owed him in prison.

"When the king heard what the slave had done, he called him in and reinstated his debt and threw the slave who had originally been forgiven into prison!

"To me, this illustrates a powerful principle that we are often unaware of. If we don't walk in forgiveness and give forgiveness, then we really can't receive forgiveness. In Matthew 18:35 Jesus says, 'This is how my Heavenly Father will treat each of you unless you forgive your brother from your heart.'

"There is a forgiveness that has to come from our hearts toward one another, not just from our minds. Mark 11:25-26 says, 'Whenever you stand praying, forgive, if you have anything against anyone, so that your Father who is in heaven will also forgive you your transgressions. But if you do not forgive, neither will your Father who is in heaven forgive your transgressions.'

"Now, we are not talking about salvation and going to heaven. I believe when you accept Jesus Christ as your Lord and Savior that you already have your 'ticket to heaven,' so to speak. In both passages, the command to forgive others is given to ones who have already been forgiven of their own sins. We can forgive others because we've been forgiven, just as we can love others because we've been loved first. When we choose not to forgive out of the forgiveness we've been given, we don't lose our eternal salvation, but it does affect the way that we walk in the provisions and the blessing of what the Father has for us here on the earth. If we choose not to forgive, it limits us and it limits God's ability to bless us with what He has predestined for us because we are walking in darkness."

Ben held up his pen and said, "I just heard a guy teaching on the radio about this passage this week. This passage really frustrated him because he was trying to explain that the one who receives Christ is forgiven, but it was hard for him to understand the 'reinstatement of debt' part of this parable. In Christ we know that our past, present, and future sins are covered by His blood. But when this radio guy read Matthew 18 you could just hear it in the way he was trying to teach that the line really threw a wrench into his rational mind."

Ben went on, "I think this guy, along with many other people, looks at Matthew 18 and sees this as a cosmic, all-inclusive 'being thrown out of salvation' moment, but we know from the Father's love that that is not what He is doing. If you don't understand God's love for you, which is what we covered in the first chapter, and you don't understand that the Father's love holds us and keeps us as sons, then this passage could tell you you're in danger of being thrown out of the Father's love. You might feel like this parable explains a new loop hole in the formula, and that if you miss this requirement right here, then the Father's love doesn't apply to you and you are not forgiven anymore—in the sense of eternal salvation.

"Like we talked about earlier," said Tim, "we know that sin and salvation are not the whole story, but when our minds are only on whether we're saved and if we belong or not, it's easy to take this passage the wrong way. I think that God, having fully accepted us eternally, is simply trying to teach us some things about life from this passage."

"It's just like any other thing that God sets up for kingdom rule," Ben added. "If you don't forgive, which is our kingdom nature as sons of God, you are going to suffer consequences in both the natural and the spiritual. As the Scripture says, whatever you bind on earth is also bound in heaven, and whatever you loose on earth is loosed in heaven. What we do or don't do here on earth has an effect in the spiritual."

Doug sipped and gestured with his cup, "I think we are going back to what we talked about in the first chapter when Tim asked the question about why God allows wars and this and that. Well, if you come from a 'son' mentality, you are going to forgive. The nature of God is not to judge and condemn because the heart of God is reconciliation. If you have the nature of Christ in you, you will reconcile and forgive. Once you recognize and are grounded in the love of the Father, then you will naturally be a reconciler."

Tim replied, "But when we're going against the grain of our true nature in the kingdom as sons of God, of course some nasty things are going to happen."

"Yes," said Ben, "and—as for the guy on the radio who struggled—the answer might be a *both-and* solution. On one hand, if you just don't have a forgiving nature you might find yourself in this parable as the one who did not have the heart of the King and was handed over to the jailers. It could be a question for your relationship with God. But on the other hand, if you love Jesus but still have trouble forgiving, then you have just been promised the same consequences in this life as anyone else who won't forgive...so we need to get serious."

"No one wants to worry about forgiving other people. Well, you don't have to worry about forgiving someone if you don't take it into account when suffered wrong," ventured Doug with delight. "That is the heart of the Father because God knows that the wrong is not who we are in Christ, it is just what we did."

Doug looked like he was ready to say something else, and Ben and Tim waited.

"I want to pull all that you two have been talking about into one clear principle: we have to forgive others," he said in summary. "Agreed?"

Ben and Tim nodded in affirmation.

"Now," said Doug, finishing his coffee and setting it aside, "let's talk about the second principle of forgiveness: *forgiving ourselves*. It's closely tied to the first principle, which is that the Father forgives us, but, like I said, we'll expand on that point even more later.

"There is a trap of the enemy that binds us in unforgiveness, and people struggle not only with forgiving others but also with forgiving themselves. When people don't understand the love of the Father or their sonship, they agree with the lies of the enemy about who they are and about whether God loves them when bad things happen to them. As a result, they make a judgment both against themselves and against the Father.

"For example, you take a young girl that has been abused by her dad or uncle growing up. Usually, then, her first boyfriend will be abusive, then her first husband as well, and then her second husband, too. Obviously, she hasn't done anything wrong to cause the abuse—she was a victim from the very beginning. However, if she doesn't know how to walk in forgiveness and recognize herself as the daughter of God that she is, the enemy has room to come in and tell her who she is, what she deserves, and who God is, too. She lives her life not only as a victim to the abuse, but also as a victim to her judgment against herself and

God. She has to forgive herself for believing the lies of the enemy in order to come into the freedom God means for her to have."

"She doesn't think she is worthy of anything better," reflected Ben.

"She can't forgive herself," replied Doug, "because she doesn't understand the love of the Father and she has judged herself saying, whether subconsciously or consciously, 'this is what I deserve.' And she goes from one bad situation to another.

"There are many believers in the Church today that are in that scenario because they don't understand the foundation of forgiveness," Doug continued. "As we've said, unforgiveness can rob and imprison us, so we need to learn how to walk in forgiveness."

Tim observed, "I think it's noteworthy the strong connection you're making between unforgiveness and bad judgments that hinder our walk. They seem to be almost inseparable."

"If we don't forgive, it robs us of our identity as sons because God's love for us is always questioned," said Doug. "If I can't forgive myself, then how can I receive God's forgiveness? If I can't forgive myself, then how can I receive your forgiveness?

"The first thing that we have to do is say 'God has forgiven me and because of that I have to forgive myself.' In fact, I would be putting myself above the Father if I couldn't forgive myself. I'd be saying, 'Well, Jesus, what you did was great, super and fine for other people, but it wasn't enough for me. You have to hang on the cross and die again because your blood wasn't sufficient enough to cover all my sins.' That is a lie of the enemy. But think of how many people are walking in that kind of bondage simply because they don't understand forgiveness.

"Look at the Lord's Prayer," Doug continued. "It says 'Our Father who art in heaven...Forgive us our debts as we have forgiven our debtors.' Well now, Jesus is saying that I should ask the Father to forgive me the way I have forgiven Ben. Forgive me the way I have forgiven Tim. Do I really want the Father to forgive me the way I have forgiven others?"

Doug paused for a smile as he does when delivering a rebuke disguised as a question.

"That is why it is important for us, I believe, to walk in an understanding of forgiveness. If I hold an offense against someone, who is being robbed of relationship with the Father? I am."

"I really dig that," responded Ben. "There is something about understanding that the blood of Christ has cosmically covered all things and has restored our relationship with Dad. That is true and there is no loophole. I just want to say that out loud again.

"And still, we are not excused or insulated in any way from the principle of forgiveness that you are teaching, Doug. If you don't forgive, there are consequences of that; it has an effect in the heavenlies. We even see that in this prayer. If you don't forgive others, there is going to be a break. There is going to be a relational reconciliation problem between you and the Father. And you still belong to Him, but there are going to be some issues in there. Our unforgiveness against someone doesn't alter the great work of salvation that Christ did in us."

"There can be some static in your relationship—hindrance in your walk—however you want to say it," Doug added. "But sooner or later the Father's love is going to show you that, 'hey dummy, I have already forgiven you in this deal by the blood of Jesus, so you don't even need to be walking with these issues; all you have to do is forgive.'

"I think John 20:23 explains what we're trying to say. It says, 'If you forgive the sins of any, they are forgiven them; if you retain the sins of any, they are retained.' Now, that tells me that if I forgive the sins of someone, their sins are forgiven. Their sins are forgiven from my heart. But if I retain the sins of someone, where are those sins retained?

"They are retained in my heart. It has nothing to do with the shed blood of Jesus or the ability for God to forgive you. It has to do with your heart. God is always forcing us to deal with our hearts so we can become more like Him."

Letting that thought persist a moment, Doug shifted in his seat from a posture of soul-piercing truth delivery to one of simple explanation. He then went on:

"See, a lot of times we let unforgiveness rule in our heart and then we reap consequences which are not healthy to our soul. Here's an example. A person has offended you, but after a while he comes and asks forgiveness, but you don't forgive him from your heart. That person starts being blessed by the Father, and all of a sudden you are thinking, 'well, God, how can you bless him? Look what he did to me.'

"Well, he is forgiven and he is God's son so it is not an issue between him and God, but it is an issue with you because you have let it take root in your heart. So now you are reaping the fruit that the sin produces because you have chosen not to forgive from your heart."

Ben spoke up, "I wonder sometimes. I have been reading a lot and studying where Jesus made that very clear principle or promise of 'whatever you bind on the earth shall be bound in heaven' and 'whatever you loose on earth shall be loosed in heaven.' And, like I mentioned earlier, I wonder if this is part of it. Whatever you don't forgive, it is as though you lasso it to the earth and you make it stick here and you give it life. By not forgiving a debt you give it life and you make it stay here and it has effects here and it has effects in heaven and it changes the spiritual atmosphere in your journey and in your life and their life. But if you forgive it, even though it's the same mistake, it is released and it leaves our atmosphere. It leaves the earth and it is loosed and it is done away with and it dies and no longer has any power."

"Yes, I think there is truth in what you're saying," Doug answered. "I have seen people that couldn't get healed and came up for prayer and the Lord gave a word of knowledge or discernment that they had unforgiveness toward somebody. And as soon as they verbalized that forgiveness and released it and blessed that person, they received their healing.

"I have seen financial situations where people were bound up with judgments and unforgiveness and as soon as they released those, finances were released to them.

"It is a principle that light and dark cannot fellowship. I think that when you choose to walk away from the understanding of what the Father has called you to be as a son and you walk away from His love and you instead hold unforgiveness in your heart, then you basically ask the devil to be your father in that situation. In effect you are agreeing with the darkness and have given the devil a key to come in and rule in that area of your life.

"Now if that's what I've done, I can rebuke the devil and I can appropriate the blood of Jesus, and nothing will happen until I verbalize that I forgive. There is power and life in the tongue, and I believe it is important when someone offends us or we offend someone that we go to them and say, 'Brother, I have offended you and I ask you to forgive me. Will you forgive me?' It breaks that oppression that we have bound ourselves up in.

"Like I said, I don't know how many times I have seen people that couldn't get delivered or get healed because of the unforgiveness in their hearts. They had made such judgments against themselves that they couldn't forgive themselves. And if they couldn't forgive themselves then how could God give them the gift of the Holy Spirit? And as soon as they forgave themselves, they were baptized in the Holy Spirit and started speaking in tongues. I think the power of unforgiveness is a stronghold that most of the people in the Church today are not aware of, and it is easy not to understand the depths of this stronghold in our lives."

Ben turned a page in his Bible and looked up. "Do you think that there is any sin other than the sin of unforgiveness that has as much far-reaching or destructive power in the lives of believers?" he asked. "As you are walking with believers and helping them grow in the Lord, is there anything that could possibly surpass the sin of unforgiveness for bringing darkness and brokenness into a believer's life?"

Doug answered, "Personally, I think that unforgiveness is probably one of the main strongholds because it binds you up in a judgment of who you are. If you don't forgive yourself of your past sins then how can you experience the love of the Father? How can you really come into an understanding of your sonship? You can't come into understanding because you are always questioning, saying, 'Well, yeah, but God really doesn't know this or that.'"

"Because you are holding your dark little view of things above God's," observed Tim.

"Yes," replied Doug, "and that is why people are so fearful to really come in to relationships and family, because when you come into family, you come into a place of being transparent where you are walking in the light as He is in the light. When you walk in the light, any darkness is exposed. People are fearful of coming into a place of relationship and commitment because they are fearful that their past is going to be found out."

Doug leaned forward as if telling the good part of a story, "Well, if I can forgive my past, then my past is part of my testimony." Then he quoted Revelation, 'And they overcame Him by the blood of the Lamb and the word of their testimony.' "See how the enemy can just rob us of relationships, destiny, purpose and even our testimony because of unforgiveness?"

Doug got up and rinsed his coffee cup, and, setting it by the sink, continued to speak. "You read Ephesians, a letter Paul is writing to the Church. These are Spirit-filled, born again, power-walking Christians that he is addressing. He says in Ephesians 4:25, 'Therefore each of you must put off falsehood and speak truthfully to his neighbor, for we are all members of one body. In your anger do not sin. Do not let the sun go down while you are still angry, and do not give the devil a foothold.'

"It says it's okay to be angry with somebody, but it also says 'don't let the sun go down on your anger.' I think when you don't forgive that person and you let the sun go down on your anger you are carrying over unforgiveness. But if you tell that person, 'Hey, I am mad at you and it wasn't right what you did but I want to forgive you.' Then see, that is walking in the light instead of giving the devil an opportunity to rule in your relationships."

"I wonder how much many of us go about so-called Christian activities while we're not seeing the whole picture because of unforgiveness and the judgments that come with it," pondered Tim.

Doug answered, "We have a Church building on every corner because most of us don't have a good foundation of walking in the light. New Church structures are often built because of division, unforgiveness and judgments: 'You didn't like what I said and you didn't like the way I did ministry, so I am going to take what God has given me and go start my own thing.'

"People who speak like this don't understand the family of God and they don't understand kingdom relationships, and so they have built a new work that is basically born out of rebellion and unforgiveness. And then they wonder why the Father hasn't brought His full blessing to what they are doing."

"You said, 'don't give the devil a foothold' in the Ephesians passage," remembered Ben. "It seemed like you were defining the devil's foothold as an opportunity or permission to come and rule or bring destruction to a relationship. Do you think the devil's foothold is mostly about breaking relationships?"

"Oh, most definitely," Doug responded, "because he ultimately wants to break my relationship with the Father. He is always questioning my wife's love for me. He is always questioning people's love around me. And he is always questioning God's love for me. If those questions or accusations find a home in my mind, I become a performer instead of being who I am. And that's what we see, people who perform to be accepted instead of being content with who they are."

"I really like defining the meaning of these statements," Ben said. "Reading that Scripture casually can have us gloss over the impact of it. We might say, 'Oh, I don't want to give the devil a foothold,' but we don't ask what that really means or what it would do to us. Tim, can you think of anything else that would fall into the 'give the devil a foothold' category other than remaining unreconciled to the Father, others, or with yourself?

"Do we need anything else?" Tim replied, opening his hands. "That seems like enough to me. I guess I can't think of anything else the devil needs to do to us. It goes back to what Doug was saying about how unforgiveness brings a judgment and allows a diminished vision of reality that's not in line with God's way of seeing things. When I think of a foothold or an opportunity in this realm, I think about allowing the devil to define the situation and tell you what is what."

"Allowing the devil to be the lord of that situation," clarified Doug.

"Exactly," said Tim. "I don't think I have heard it said that way before. I liked how you expressed the idea that forgiveness allows us to overcome that. When unforgiveness and the judgments that come from it are dealt with, we have our minds renewed so we know what is what. We walk in faith and we can come into destiny instead of being in this small visage where the devil is able to define who we are and what the situation is."

"You just turned a light bulb on in my mind," said Ben enthusiastically. "If unforgiveness gives the devil a foothold and forgiveness closes his opportunity then it means that the devil is simply looking for an opportunity, a grip by which he can break down family and break down relationships. *That's his mission.* People who are expecting the devil's foothold to be some sort of supernatural expression of weirdness need to understand that the devil's primary goal is to destroy our relationships with God, ourselves, and others, not just to cause us to fear what is under the bed. What we are saying is that forgiveness heals and protects those relationships from the mission of the devil. This says a lot about the priority of the Father in our lives and that forgiveness really is foundational to our journey."

Doug continued, "So then consider where it says that no weapon formed against you will prosper and no plan against you will succeed, and that God has given us all power and authority to rule. If all of that is true, and if the Scripture that says that the devil is under our feet is true—and I believe the word is true—

then what gives the devil the authority to rule in our lives? What is the door that opens that up? Unforgiveness. In II Corinthians 2:10-11, Paul says, 'But to the one whom you forgive anything, I forgive also. For indeed what I have forgiven if I have forgiven anything I did it for your sake in the presence of Christ so that no advantage would be taken of us by Satan, for we are not ignorant of his schemes.'"

"The way he talks there," observed Tim, "Paul seems to take it for granted as an obvious fact that unforgiveness tears relationships apart, and that it is the devil himself who is taking advantage of us when that happens."

"Unforgiveness is such a powerful tool," Doug reinforced. "As an example, Tim and Ben are such good friends and I am good friends with them, too. If Tim takes an offense at Ben over some issue, but I side with Ben and say, 'Tim, you are wrong in this deal.' What happens?"

Doug paused to allow the scenario to sink in.

"Then, not only has Ben's relationship with Tim been stolen, but my relationship with Tim has been stolen, too. So how did that happen? The enemy has come in and found a foothold because I chose a side and made a judgment.

"Here's another case: Let's say that Tim does something to Ben and then Ben gets mad. I take up Ben's offense and say, 'Yeah, Tim, you shouldn't have done that. That wasn't right.' Pretty soon Ben and Tim get reconciled by forgiving one another but now that I have taken up Ben's offense, I still haven't forgiven anyone. So now, I am robbed of my relationship with both Ben and Tim because now I am mad at both. I am mad at Tim for the original offense, and I am mad at Ben, too, because 'How could Ben be so dumb to forgive Tim for what he did? It was so wrong.'

"Nothing was really done to me. I had just taken up an offense and adopted someone else's unforgiveness."

Ben jumped in and said, "Boy, when you say it like that—when you have given the devil an opportunity to come and work in a relationship and define the nature of things, it helps me understand why taking up somebody else's offense is deadly! It is one of the hardest things to help someone get over or to get over myself."

Tim agreed, "It feels so righteous to be a defender. We want to be a defender of people who are hurting. We don't understand, however, that it can lead to its own form of unforgiveness."

"We need to know when the devil is in a situation, creating the atmosphere of division," Ben posited. "You can walk right in with a good heart but still step right in the middle of a trap when you take up someone else's offense. It is hard to get that stuff from around your ankles."

"I guess that's one reason why we're always called to be reconcilers, not judges and dividers of the good from the evil," Tim said.

Doug chuckled. "Well, as you may have noticed over the years, I have learned that when I am in a relationship with different people and things happen like that, they say, 'Whose side are you going to take?' And I say, 'I am going to take God's side.'

"They say, 'Well, that is not fair!' and I say, 'Well, God is not fair. God is a righteous God.' He's not a fair God, but a righteous God.

"If I'm walking with Tim and a situation arises where Ben offends Tim, I don't deal with the thing Ben did to Tim. I deal with Tim's heart to forgive Ben. Tim might say, 'Well, Ben did it. Deal with his heart,' but I say, 'Well, yeah, but what Ben does is not the issue right now. I have to guard your heart and make sure your heart is healthy in this because if you allow unforgiveness to come in, then you have opened up an opportunity for the devil to come in and rule.'

"So in a relationship, I have a responsibility to help someone guard his heart. And that is basically what it talks about in Hebrews. It says to submit to those who watch over your soul. It doesn't say to submit to those who lord over your faith. No man is supposed to lord over your faith. But we need people to help watch over our souls because our souls are what the enemy attacks. So when we are ministering to people about forgiveness, we have to make sure that the person's heart is right to forgive an offender, whether or not the offender ever admits they're wrong or forgives as well."

"I like that Scripture reference because it clearly speaks of the role of leaders as helping people keep their hearts healthy," affirmed Tim. "Well, everyone can be a leader to someone, and here it even says that if we don't do this heart-care for the people we lead, we have to give an account as to why not!"

Ben had been making some notes in the margin of his journal and took this opportunity to ask some questions: "Just as a footnote, Doug. When you say 'watch over someone's soul,' how do you define that? What is a person's soul?"

"I believe the soul, in the simplest definition, is your mind, your will, and your emotions," Doug answered. "Where does the devil attack us?" He asked the question only to answer it himself: "Our souls.

"For example," he continued, "he attacks us a lot in our minds. We'll talk more about this later, but for now, how does him attacking us in our minds work in terms of unforgiveness? Well, he brings a thought into your mind: 'You know, Ben did something to you and you didn't deserve that.' And you start to think, 'Yeah, I didn't deserve that. Ben shouldn't have done that.' All of a sudden, what does that start producing? An unforgiveness in your heart that agrees with the thought the devil put in your mind. We need people—brothers, sisters, fathers and mothers in the Lord—that will come in and say, 'Hey, you are kind of being manipulated through your soul here. You need to rule that thought.'"

"So, Doug," Ben interrupted, "defining the soul, you said 'mind, will and emotions.' These are sort of the earthly elements of a person's exchange and expression, right?"

Tim chimed in while Doug started turning pages in his Bible: "Yes, somewhat synonymous with 'flesh,' in the Scriptures. When I first started translating Doug's messages into Spanish, that point confused me for a while until I understood that soul is different than spirit. You hear people talk about 'saving souls' when it might be more accurate to speak about people's spirits in that context—the eternal part of us that is united with God's Spirit when we're saved. For me, when I began to understand my soul as more earthly and connected to my flesh, the idea of ruling it made more sense."

"Like Tim said," agreed Doug, "when you accept Jesus Christ as your Savior, your spirit is born again. Your spirit becomes alive again but your soul is in the process of being saved. We have to rule our souls.

"I wish that when I accepted Jesus Christ as my Lord and Savior and got baptized in the Holy Ghost that everything was taken care of. But it wasn't. Well, it was in an eternal sense, but it wasn't in a temporal sense. I have to now appropriate in the temporal that which was taken care of in the eternal. Part of watching for someone's soul is helping them come into the purpose and the call of the grace of God on them to fulfill their destiny."

"And, so, helping someone to forgive is the key to a pastoral role if you are really going to be watching after someone or helping somebody in their journey," affirmed Ben.

"If you look at the Scripture," said Doug, "we are to forgive one another as God forgave us in Christ. How did God forgive us in Christ? Even while I was yet a sinner, God made provision for me to be forgiven. I wasn't looking for the Lord when He found me. When He did find me, I said to myself 'I need to get in on this deal' so I repented and started to change.

"This is that first principle we mentioned at the beginning of this chapter: the Father forgives our sins. All my failures and all my sins were already covered in Christ Jesus; I was forgiven before I even accepted forgiveness. But until I accepted forgiveness I couldn't appropriate that forgiveness. As God's word talks about in Ezekiel, it is God's heart that none should perish but all should come to be saved. That is His heart, but there are a lot of people that die and go to hell. Why? Not because God doesn't want them to know Him, it is because they chose not to appropriate the provision that the Father gave them."

Doug had left his notes at this point completely and was engaging the discussion with full hand gestures.

"What is that provision that the Father gave them? Calling on the name of the Lord so that they may be saved. As a son, I have all these things the Father has given me and they are mine to walk in. But if I don't appropriate them, is that the Father's fault? No, it is our fault because we have chosen not to rule in that situation."

"So to say it another way, to appropriate a blessing or a provision is to live like it's real with my mind, will, and emotions, because it is," said Tim, tapping the masonite table with a knuckle for emphasis. "Sometimes we take a truth in the Scripture, like 'seek first the kingdom of God and His righteousness and all these things will be added unto you' and we try to honor it. But later we find ourselves saying 'but in the real world, you only get what you work for.'"

Tim continued, "but what you're saying about appropriation is helping me understand that anything God speaks in the Scripture is true. God is not a liar. The principles He lays out are as real as the physical world he spoke into existence. So a provision He makes is more true than some of what I may see with the lens of my human experience—my soul. And if I don't see blessings that the Scriptures speak of in my own life, it's probably because I'm not walking in faith that they are mine, or because I have some hang-up or judgment going on. So appropriating God's provision is to change my mind and make the other parts of my soul submit to the truth, in order not to leave all the blessings for the eternal. That stirs up faith in me to walk in eternal truths here and now."

"It's up to us to appropriate what God has first spoken," Doug nodded. "That is why God has called us to rule and not to react. Most of us react in our walk instead of ruling in our walk. We react to the circumstances: if someone loves me then I love them. If someone does good to me then I will do good to them. If someone does bad to me, then I will do bad to them. That is the way of a reactor.

"But the principles Jesus gives us in Matthew 5 show what it's like to be a ruler: when someone does evil to you then you bless them. If someone slaps you on the right cheek then you turn your left cheek. If someone asks for your shirt then you give them your coat too. Why? We are ruling and appropriating the provision of what the Father says is ours to walk in and to exercise in His kingdom, no matter the circumstance."

Ben looked out the window and saw some new campers setting up nearby. "I had a guy write me this week and he said, 'Could you define for me what it really means to lay foundations? You say that apostles lay foundations.' What we're talking about now really answers his question. As people read this book, they are reading foundational teachings. These are not new foundations; they are just digging down to the basics, digging down to Jesus. Jesus is the foundation, period."

"Yes, He is *the* sure foundation," acknowledged Doug.

Ben added for clarity, "But if you don't learn how to appropriate and really function in what Christ has brought to you as a gift—the gift of forgiveness, for instance—then you are not receiving all that He came to bring you. In other words, you are not walking on *the* foundation. So you could know Jesus and walk with Him as a believer, but you need to learn to live your life on the foundations of His kingdom—the way things really are in Christ."

Doug nodded and replied, "If you look at the world today, especially in religious systems, the apostolic and prophetic are two gifts that aren't easily received. Why? Because the apostles and prophets lay the foundations with Jesus Christ being the chief cornerstone. That is why the devil does so much to resist the apostolic and prophetic ministry released to the body of Christ today—because they lay foundation. The foundation of forgiveness, the foundation of love, and the foundation of faith.

"You look today and ninety percent of what is being taught to the Church is basically 'you need to quit sinning and get saved or you are going to hell.' Well, like I said in the first chapter, the reason I confessed my sin and repented and received Jesus is so I could go to heaven. But that is not God's ultimate goal for me. Even though I'm saved I'm still walking around on the earth, so evidently he has something else for me to do. God's ultimate goal is that I be reinstated to fulfill my destiny that God has predestined for me to accomplish in Christ here on the earth."

"That is why I want everybody to read this book," smiled Ben.

"Yeah," Tim concurred. "I think that is a part of what it means to reign with Christ. We could receive the complete work of Christ in our spirits and yet know little of God's goodness and just escape condemnation as a man through the flames. This is a picture the apostle Paul used which refers to people who have a foundation but nothing good built on it.

"But if we reign with Christ, building something that will last on the foundation of Jesus, we appropriate this completeness and we make it visible in the ways that we live our lives and the ways that we relate to each other. We really bring about an understanding of who God is in things that are tangible—things that we can touch and see and point to—which really brings glory to the Father.

"Ruling and reigning and appropriating God's blessings are 'right now' activities," Tim continued. "We don't let the story be just about sin, and—oh, yeah—the final unread chapter called *eternity*. Instead, we bring the purposes of eternity and an understanding of the Father's heart into the frontal frame of the story that we are in right now."

Ben shifted gears. "It is exciting to me, Doug, to hear you talking about this. Because this means that forgiveness is more than just teaching on some relationship rules that we ought to follow. This is really understanding that to come into your destiny as a son and to enjoy what Christ has really done for us in bringing us back to the Father is to live this life of forgiveness. In it we begin to enjoy a type of power and authority and joy that we couldn't have any other way."

Doug nodded and continued, "In Luke 6:27 it says, 'And I say to you who hear, love your enemies, do good to those who hate you, bless those who curse you, and pray for those who mistreat you.' What is the foundation of that? Forgiveness! You can't do that in your flesh. That is what we are talking about. We are not human beings encountering spiritual things. We are spiritual beings encountering human things.

"What are some of these human things? Immorality, impurity, sensuality, idolatry, sorcery, enmities, strife, jealousy, outbursts of anger, disputes, dissensions, factions, envying, drunkenness, carousing, and things like that are all of the flesh. But we are not ruled by them because we are walking in the Spirit and we are merely encountering those things. We are not distracted by them.

"Why?

"Because we are appropriating the foundations of who we are in Christ and we are blessing those that curse us. We are doing good to those who hate us."

"Those who find themselves in the acts of the flesh," said Tim.

"Yes, and because of that," continued Doug, "the Bible says it is like heaping coals upon their heads. When someone comes up that is really mad at me and I say, 'Brother, you are right. I am sorry. Forgive me.' It takes away the authority and the power they have about what I did. When I humble myself before a brother, he has no other case. Then if he chooses to pursue it any further, he is only giving the devil an opportunity to rule and to bring condemnation and judgments."

Tim wrote furiously in his notebook again. "So we see there an example of someone who is not responding to humility and a request for forgiveness. What else would you say to people who want to be able to discern well between the Lord using someone who is bringing a loving rebuke to you about an issue, and someone who's got their own hang-up and is just causing division?"

Doug considered the question for a moment, and then answered, "The Bible talks in Romans 12 about how there is now therefore no condemnation for those that are in Christ Jesus. See, God will never deal with us through condemnation. Anytime we are battling condemnation, it is because we are walking in the flesh because in Christ there is no condemnation. Now, there is conviction. God will convict us of our sin and God will chasten us in our sin but He will never condemn us in our sin."

Ben chimed in, "I'd like to think together some more on that idea of being spiritual beings dealing with human things, not human beings dealing with spiritual things. That is a really powerful saying. Just to clarify, would you say that human things are synonymous with soulish things?"

"I think the human things are everything that is temporal," said Doug. "That is, what we taste, see, and feel; they are the things that we feel like we have to have in our own strength. However, the heart of God is not selfish. We read in the Bible that God loves us extravagantly. It pleases the Father to give us His kingdom. It says don't worry about these temporal things. Don't worry about what you should eat and what you should put on, what you should do. The Father knows you have need of those things but seek first His kingdom because it pleases the Father to give us His kingdom. A lot of times if we don't understand that it pleases the Father to give us freely these things, then we strive to earn them.

"He has given us Christ. He has given us faith. He has given us the Holy Spirit. He has given us all these things so we can exercise our right as His sons on the earth to bring forth His kingdom. But what happens is that we start seeking things. We start saying, 'What will I eat? What will I wear?' And we forget to seek the kingdom. In seeking things we are always going to be in need, but in seeking Him we are always going to be in abundance. We'll go into that further later, though."

It was getting late in the day now. The new campers nearby had pitched their tent and were starting a fire. Ben, undistracted from the conversation, watched afternoon shadows that were already advancing into the campsite. He said, still staring out the window, "When you read the Ephesians passage, there were two things noted in there. One is the idea of giving the devil a foothold, and the other is the idea of time: 'Don't let the sun go down on your anger.' Are you going to make some notes on the time restraints on forgiveness?"

Doug answered, "In my life, and especially in the last few years, I know when I sin. Someone doesn't have to tell me, 'hey you sinned there.' I know when I sin. When I sin, I have to violate everything that has been in me for the last thirty-five years. It violates the word of God. It violates the character and nature of the Father. It violates the Holy Spirit. It violates everything within me; I have to choose to sin.

"There has never been a time when I choose to let the dumb spirit get on me and do something dumb that I don't know that I have done a dumb thing. The Holy Spirit is always there to convict me. Part of the job of the Holy Spirit is to convict us of sin. He is to make known the things that the Father has for us, to reveal the things Christ did for us, and to convict us. So, if we are walking as a son, and walking in the understanding of the love of the Father, the Father is always going to be quick to respond to us. It doesn't get difficult as long as we obey when the Holy Spirit says, 'Hey that was a dumb thing you did. This is the way over here.' But what keeps us from repenting sometimes is pride. We try to hide our errors, saying to ourselves, 'what will they think if they knew I made a mistake there?'"

Tim agreed. "Then we're walking in darkness, hiding one thing and then another."

"So we have to humble ourselves. That is why it says unless you humble yourself as a little child, you can't enter into the kingdom," Doug said.

"How else does a little child act?" Doug asked. "She just believes what she hears. A little child doesn't question what her father says. She just receives it and enters in. It says we have to have childlike faith; we just receive what the word says and what the Holy Spirit speaks to us. So if the Holy Spirit convicts me about something, I need to be quick to respond and say, 'Hey, Ben, I am sorry brother, I didn't realize what I did to you, but that was bad.'

"The more we walk in sonship and the more we walk in maturity of what God has worked in us, then the quicker we are to repent."

"It is our nature as sons to forgive quickly because we don't like unreconciled relationships," Ben observed. "It is just not in our nature to not desire family. And that is an important value. If you don't value family, then why should you be in a hurry to reconcile it? But if you value family and you value other people and your relationship with the Father, you want to be quick to forgive because you are trying to let that value system be number one for you. I wish that all the sons that read this could see this working so that they can bust the myth that *time heals*. Who invented that?"

"The devil did," said Doug, answering the rhetorical question to Ben's surprise, "because he wants us to stay in time because that is all he can rule in. However, in God there is no time. A day is as a thousand years and a thousand years is as a day. With God, there is no beginning and no end. If you get that concept you can understand why it says 'don't let the sun go down on your anger.' We know when the sun rises and when the sun goes down. God put that in there for us because we need to know that forgiveness is something that needs to be done the day the offense happens so that the enemy has no time to come in and influence us."

Doug continued, "Okay, I am to forgive you the way that God forgave me in Christ. God forgave me in Christ without any conditions. God forgave me of my sin in Christ Jesus even if I never asked Him. Now, I can't appropriate the benefit of being forgiven if I don't confess my sins. But my sins are still forgiven. God paid the price for my sins whether I ever respond to it or not. There are a lot of people that die and go to hell whose sin had been forgiven but who never appropriated that forgiveness by receiving it."

"I know some people that have had a real problem learning that the receiving part is necessary," said Ben. "It is a real struggle for the modern mind to understand that in Christ all are forgiven and that availability is there. Yet, all might not receive it and so they make it useless."

Doug looked up in thought briefly. "That brings to mind another thing. Our mannerisms should not be a stumbling block to people in the day of their visitation," he said. "If I am not walking in the character and the nature of the Father and someone has been watching and observing how I walk, well then on the day of their visitation they might think, 'Well, if that is what it is to be a Christian, I do not want to do that. He is just as big a hypocrite as I am.'

"That is why it is important for us to walk as children of our Heavenly Father, because when people watch us and the Holy Spirit draws them, they can say, 'Oh yeah, that is what it is to be a Christian. That is what it is to be a son. I want to be like that.'"

Barely inhaling he continued, "We don't know who is watching and we can be a stumbling block and a hindrance to someone if we do not walk in what God has called us to walk in. And there again it is because we choose not to forgive. It is sad to say but there is a lot more covenant in some situations in the world than there is covenant in the Church. Sinners come into agreement sometimes and covenant in sin. You have different organizations, different groups..."

"Committing together, staying together," interrupted Ben.

"Many organizations have stayed together because they have made a covenant to sin," said Doug, slowing down a bit. "They made a covenant to not forgive an offense. When we do that we are a stumbling block to people and they don't want to be like us because we are hypocritical, judgmental, angry and bitter. We have got all that dark stuff working around us because we have chosen not to appropriate the benefits of the kingdom."

"It is strange to think that corporate unforgiveness is sometimes the glue that holds a group together. I mean, all those things you just talked about were just unforgiveness issues— weren't they?" asked Ben.

"Yes," answered Doug. "That is why I think unforgiveness is a powerful tool that the devil uses to discredit our testimony to the world. In one Scripture it talks about when the world sees us loving one another the world is going to know that God sent His Son. What does it mean to love one another? Covering one another. Taking care of one another and nourishing one another, supporting one another, honoring one another. And when the world sees us doing that, which is the heart of the Father, they are going to say, 'Hey, I want that.'"

Tim agreed. "I'd like to point out that this is a totally different attitude than what you hear sometimes as it relates to our *testimony*. We often hear, 'You better behave because you are representing Jesus. Pretend you are better than you are—or that your life is better than it is—because the world is watching!'"

Tim's tone became more serious, "But what we're talking about here is not striving and masquerading. If the world sees us in a dysfunctional family that is full of unforgiveness, then…well, nobody needs another one of those."

"Yeah, we have plenty of that to go around," said Ben.

Doug laughed. "Especially when they are told, 'If you come join us you are going to have to start giving tithes and offerings.' Now it is even going to cost them money to join!"

Now all three were laughing. "People know they can get dysfunction for free," Tim said, holding his hands up as if weighing the options on scales. "I can be dysfunctional on my own for free," weighing one hand, "or I can be dysfunctional in your group and have to pay for it," weighing the other hand. "Hmmm, I wonder which they will choose?"

Ben cleaned his glasses and measured his words as he spoke, "This may be a side bar, but it seems to me that when I walk into places where believers are, one of the ways that I can tell whether or not people are living as sons and whether or not there is kingdom life in that place is the way that they relate to one another. Are they reconciled and really committed? Is there a lot of love and openness and forgiveness? It is pretty easy to sense dysfunction when you walk into a room and see that people there are full of ideas and doctrine and teaching and systems and styles and ways of doing things but have no real connection between them.

"It is funny because a healthy group and an immature group might be sharing the same teachings and have the same doctrines posted on the wall. They might both be all over John 3:16, but in one group you can get a sense that they are open to one another and in love, but the other group is isolated from one another and an awkward tension prevails. I think a lot of people go into fellowships like the latter one and they feel that tension and they just have to ask, 'Is that is Christianity? That is what it means to know the Lord?'"

Doug agreed. "I Peter 3:8-12 talks about not returning evil for evil or insult for insult, but giving a blessing instead. It says not to curse because 'you were called so that you may inherit a blessing.' So the enemy can rob us from the blessings of the Lord if we are returning evil for evil, returning judgment for judgment and insult for insult. That keeps us from inheriting the blessing that the Father has for us as sons. But how do you inherit a blessing? By giving a blessing."

"Hmmm," said Ben, "if you want to inherit a blessing, give one. That is a good one."

Doug continued, "If you are having financial needs, you might send someone an offering, because the word says give because God loves a cheerful giver. I have found in my own life that if I am going through a tough time, I look to bless somebody. Because I know if I bless them, I know that the Father is going to bless me. That is His nature. Is that manipulating God? No, that is appropriating His benefits."

"It is acting like who we are: not manipulating, but appropriating," Ben observed.

Tim leaned forward again. "This is another place where you can't really build a rule or a formula. We don't want to construct a law out of this principle and then trust in it. But if you understand this principle in its proper place, bathed in the understanding of God's love and us being family, then I think that is really cool to begin to move in faith like that."

Ben looked around. "I know what you are saying because some people can take something like that in Scripture and believe that they will get a new car if they throw enough money at the right Jesus project. I think it is one of the more ridiculous applications of that Scripture ever, but it is because their value system didn't start with God's love and understanding of His family. They didn't have the right foundations."

"Now, take that concept that we are talking about," said Doug. "Once you understand the foundation of God's love, once you understand the foundation of God's forgiveness, then it brings a whole new light to the Scriptures 'For the eyes of the Lord move to and fro throughout the earth that He may strongly support those whose heart is completely His,' and 'No eye has seen, no ear has heard, no mind has conceived what God has prepared for those who love Him.'

"God deals with our hearts, and when our hearts are completely the Father's, our minds can't even imagine all that God has for us. Our eyes haven't beheld all that God has for those whose heart is completely His. So it is a heart issue. If I don't believe that God loves me in my heart and I don't have the foundation of forgiveness in my heart, then I am not going to be able to come in to the fullness of all that He has for me.

"We haven't even scratched the surface of the blessings that are ready for us, and I think that is why the enemy attacks us so much. He wants to keep us from fulfilling the destiny that God has for us in Christ.

"Proverbs 13:22 says 'a sinner's wealth is stored up for the righteous.' We haven't seen that released yet, because our hearts have not been right. We haven't seen some of the promises that God has spoken to us. Why? Because we would misappropriate them because our hearts are not wholly His. That is why God deals with our hearts. That is why someone who is watching for our soul in things of the Lord always deals with our heart. Because 'out of the heart, the mouth speaketh.'"

"You are speaking King James," Ben noted with a smile.

Doug smiled, too.

Tim ignored them and reasoned, "So if I'm watching over your soul, I could try to correct you in everything you say and do, but if I didn't help address your heart issues, it would be a never-ending task."

"But look what happens with our words when our heart is to forgive," Doug said excitedly. "In Romans, it says 'Bless those who persecute you. Bless and do not curse. Do not be overcome by evil but overcome evil with good.' How do you overcome evil with good? By releasing forgiveness. By releasing blessings. By speaking, 'I bless you brother. I'm not cursing you.'"

"It is as simple as speaking, isn't it?" responded Tim. "I don't have to call a witch doctor to curse someone or a priest to bless them, do I? I just speak good or speak evil. I always think of the Spanish for those words. *Bless* is *bendecir* which means to speak well, while *curse* is *maldecir* which means to speak badly or to speak evil."

Doug added, "I have a friend, Michael O'Shields, who has a book called *Rethinking Forgiveness*. He says that when people curse or offend you, there is a very simple thing you can do. Just forgive them and send them a blessing. That way the next time you see that person, you don't remember the offense they did. You remember the blessing you gave.

"That is how God sees us. When He sees us, He doesn't see us as the unrighteous sinner we were. He sees us as a forgiven son in Christ Jesus through the gift that He gave us. God sees us through the gift and the provision that He has given us, not through who we were before. That is learning how to forgive the way that God in Christ forgave us."

Doug held out his hand and placed a pencil in it.

"There is a simple prayer that I have seen work time and time again. When I teach this at different places, I will tell them to just put something in their hands like this—a napkin, a pencil, or whatever is around. I tell them, 'what you are holding in your hand is your right that you think you have to your judgments and your right you think you have to your unforgiveness.'

"Then I lead them through a prayer where they say, 'Father, I see that I have this judgment and that I have this unforgiveness, and I now see it as sin. I release my right to this judgment and to this unforgiveness. I choose to forgive. I ask you to appropriate the blood of Jesus and stop the reaping of this sin in my life.'

"Then I have them release the item that is in their hand."

He dropped the pencil on the floor.

"I have seen the power of God set people free and do all kinds of things because they have taken back the authority that they had given the devil by holding unforgiveness and judgment. They had allowed the devil to be god in that situation, but there was a change in the spiritual when they chose to confess and release it, to stop the reaping of what they had been sowing. I would encourage everyone to ask the Holy Spirit to search their hearts to see if there is any unforgiveness that needs to be addressed and not to delay."

EXERCISING FAITH

Having found the mostly reassembled spin-casting rod and reel a permanent home in the underbelly of the RV, Tim turned immediately to his trusted fly-fishing outfit. He hurriedly tied a #16 elk-hair caddis fly pattern onto the end of his nearly invisible tippet.

"You look quite a bit more at home with that one," Doug said, settling into a camp chair after dinner.

Ben watched the bright sky of daytime fade to deep blue while he untied his canoe from the top of the 4Runner. "She's ready for her maiden voyage."

Tim and Ben put their fishing stuff in the boat and hoisted it up onto their shoulders. "Ready to do this for a quarter mile?" he asked Tim, who glanced at the treetops, which would soon be in the shadow of the mountain.

"Hope so. Let's do it."

Moments later their feet were slipping on the loose gravel of the steep path to the reservoir. Good moods intact, they laughed and coordinated their shifting of the canoe in order to distribute the load to different muscles about every 100 yards.

"Evening comes in the woods before it comes in the campground," said Tim with an equal mix of humor and trepidation.

Ben turned his headlamp on. "There's a root here. Don't trip…"

Ben timed his advice to help Tim, who was about five steps behind him holding the back of the boat, trying in vain to see around the canoe to the beam of LED that was dancing in front of Ben on the path. "Step down now. There are one, two, three rocks to use as stairs before it flattens out."

Tim made his way awkwardly according to Ben's direction.

"You okay?" Ben responded to some shuffling of feet behind him.

"It will be worth it if the trout are biting. If not I hope you can carry this boat back up alone," kidded Tim.

Meanwhile Doug built a fire and enjoyed some time alone listening to the wind in the trees and the laughter and songs from the nearby camps. The sky was black and bursting with stars when he finally saw his companions re-appear in the warm circle of the campfire's light.

"How did it go?" asked Doug.

"Well, our hands smell all gross and fishy now," Ben answered in pretend disappointment.

"Pretty good then!" celebrated Doug.

Tim explained how quiet it was on the lake, as all the daytime hip-hop fisherman and mountain bikers had gone home, and how most everyone else must have been eating s'mores, leaving a private heaven of dry-fly fishing for rainbows from the canoe.

When everything was put away and Ben and Tim entered the RV, Doug was sitting at the table. He wasted no time as they took their seats and gathered their things.

"The next foundation in our life that we need is *faith.* Hebrews 11:1 says, 'Faith is the assurance of things hoped for and the conviction of things not seen.' Let's break that down into two parts.

"First there is the *assurance of things hoped for.* If we see that faith is a title deed of the things that the Lord has for us, or ownership of what God has predestined for us to have in Christ, then it is like when you go out and buy a vehicle. They give you a title. If you pay cash for it, the title is a clear title in your name. You own it. It is yours to do with what you want.

"Our eternal destiny is something that God has already paid for and given to us completely and freely. We have ownership of it by faith. We have the title deed to it. Faith is the title to our ownership."

Tim thumbed through his Bible, landing on the book of Hebrews. Ben listened carefully as Doug continued.

"Secondly, concerning faith, there is the *evidence of things not seen.* This is faith in action; it is the living substance that gives concrete form to what we have in Christ. It gives body to what couldn't otherwise be seen—it shows to be true what we believe.

"So, we put these two ideas together: faith is the title deed of the things we hope for and the evidence of the things not seen. I think we miss out on a lot of what God has for us because we really don't take ownership of that which God has freely given us in Christ, and not truly claiming it, how can we make it evident in our lives? When we take ownership of it, then it is ours and we can do whatever we want with it.

"In Hebrews 11:6 it says, 'Now without faith it is impossible to please Him for he who comes to God must believe that He is and that He is a rewarder of those that seek Him.' The problem is that we don't take ownership of what God has given us and we really don't believe who He is.

"It says that when we come to Him, we must first *believe that He is.* We have to come to an understanding of who He is—that He is our Father or daddy. He is someone who has given us our inheritance, paid for with the blood of His son, Christ Jesus. Only when we believe that He is can we take ownership of what He has given to us.

"It goes on and says that 'He is a rewarder of those that seek Him.' Now what is the reward of believing that He is when you seek Him?"

"Finding Him," answered Tim.

"When you come believing that He is and that He is a rewarder of those that seek Him, then the reward is obtaining the fullness of who He is," affirmed Doug. "When we obtain the fullness of who He is, then we obtain the fullness of all that He has. He has given us faith to take ownership to believe in who He is and to walk in the rewards that He has for us."

"Do you think that is the gift of faith that it talks about when the Bible says He gives us faith?" Ben asked.

"If you are referring to what it says in Romans 12 about how God has given to each a measure of faith...well, that is an interesting Scripture because it is talking about each of our function in the body," explained Doug. "It talks about how our gifts differ according to the grace given to us, and that each of us is to exercise them accordingly. And it tells us not to think more highly of ourselves than we should but to have a sober understanding of who we are because God has given each of us a measure of faith.

"If we walk in that grace and in the giftings that God has given us, if we exercise the faith that He has given us, we will establish the things that He has called us to establish on the earth. And we are not to be caught up in ourselves because it's only by His grace and the faith that He has released in us that we can accomplish what He has predestined for us in Christ. So a simple definition of faith that I like is 'calling out of eternity that which Christ has already accomplished for us and making it known here in our time.'"

"So you think it covers both the faith to receive God for who He really is and the faith to accomplish kingdom work in the earth? Or do you see them as two separate things?" asked Ben.

"I think that God gives us faith to believe in Jesus Christ and His finished work of the cross for salvation. Then as we exercise that faith to believe who He is and obtain who He is, then we are going to accomplish what He has called us to do," Doug said as plainly as if he were talking about breakfast cereal.

Ben nodded in understanding and said, "This sounds a little different than the faith that a lot of Christians and, frankly, non-Christians have teaching in their minds about. Faith is often seen as some sort of Christian voodoo. It is the amount which you can believe that you can bend metal spoons with your mind, or the amount that you can believe that you can get a bigger house, or the amount that you can believe that you won't get sick. Whatever it is, it is believing for particular things. I don't know if in that definition—call it the pop definition of faith—we are having faith to receive God for all that He is to us. There is a disconnect."

Doug responded, "Well, if you believe that He is and that He is a rewarder those who seek Him, then if I need healing it is available. If I need a home, it is available. Whatever I need, God knows my need. That is why it says it pleases the Father to give you these things. But Jesus said not to worry about those things, but to seek first His kingdom."

"So if I'm trying to stir up faith to receive a particular object or outcome, my attention might be misplaced," asserted Tim, "but faith for who God is and the rewards He might be waiting to pour out is powerful. Isn't that another way to talk about seeking His kingdom and His order, rather than trying to get His power behind my order and my personal will?"

"Yes," agreed Doug, "seeking His kingdom is seeking Him. It's walking in a relationship with Him. Then all these other things will be added to you. When I exercise faith to believe who He is, then because of who He is, He gives me the things that I need on the earth. But on the other hand, if I seek God for things, then I just get things."

"If that," Tim interjected.

"But if I seek God for who He is then I have God," Doug continued, "and when I have God, I have all of His promises. When God spoke to Abraham saying "I will surely give you a son," Abraham got impatient waiting for the promise to come about and acted in his flesh, which produced Ishmael.

"We're the same way when God meets us. The problem is, in our flesh we get our Ishmael. See, it took faith for Abraham to conceive and have Isaac. He had to believe God for what He said and he had to believe God for who He was. And when he believed God for who He was, he obtained the promise of what God had for him. The blessing was with Ishmael but the covenant was with Isaac. The blessing doesn't have the covenant; the covenant has the blessing."

"We do that so much," Tim recognized. "We have a sense that God has great blessings in store for us, but we ask him to bless what we've already laid hold of or what we're already doing, when God wants to birth something new for us."

"Doug, are you saying that Abraham's trust in the end wasn't just in his faith to get a son, but that it was in seeking the Father?" Ben questioned.

Excited, Doug replied, "He believed God! Your faith is in the object of your trust. Do you think of faith as your capacity to believe…or is it your trust in the Father Himself? The mechanics of those thoughts and the fruit that grows in those gardens are dramatically different.

"I think that ties in to Romans 10:17 where it says 'faith comes by hearing, and hearing by the word of Christ.' If faith comes from hearing the word Christ speaks, then we can have a lot of capacity to believe but if we are not having a relationship with Christ, how are we going to be able to hear those things that He has predestined for us?"

"And how can we take hold of them by faith? We can't," affirmed Tim. "So faith has to be rooted in relationship and in what God speaks. You don't shoot it wherever your soul wants to like some kind of crazy gunslinger."

"That's right," said Doug. "It comes back to relationship and family. It says not to even give thought to our earthly needs because our Father knows our needs. We are to seek first His kingdom. I think people get sidetracked in the 'name it and claim it' and in 'putting out fleece' for this and that. It's much better just resting in the assurance that my Father knows the needs I have and He already has provided for my needs. All I have to do is tap into the provision that He has for me by faith."

Ben leaned toward Doug. "Let me ask you this in full view of what you just said. The whole 'name and claim it' deal had a great hue about it in the beginning, because we were trying to learn that we could trust the Father's heart for us and therefore His provision. But the carnal mind shifted a lot and turned it into a formula, and people trusted in their trust in order to have something. They just forgot that the Father was even in the deal.

"But this other thing you said about 'putting out fleece,' now this is a different animal and I wonder if you know where this comes from or how people got to this? I have some friends who the Father had already spoken to about making a move to a new city. They were already saying that they were comfortable to make this move, but then...they said that they were going to meet with this prophetic guy and 'put out the fleece.' In other words, they were looking for a sign. Where does that idea come from?"

Doug sighed, "There is some scriptural basis for that in Judges 6, but I think what you're talking about sometimes comes from immaturity in hearing. We want to be able to fail and then blame someone else instead of having to wrestle with our own intimacy with the Father. It's like Y2K, where people were telling everyone to store up everything and everyone was just going along with it, but few seemed to be seeking the Lord for themselves."

"Yeah, a lot of Christians needed beans and guns in 1999. There was no problem coming up with an escape clause for that," said Tim.

Doug laughed and said, "Someone told me that he decided they needed to store up supplies for thirty days. I asked, 'What happens after thirty days if you run out?' He said, 'Then we have to exercise faith.' I asked him, 'Why not go into it with faith right away instead of waiting thirty days and then realizing you need faith?'

"I would just as soon go into it having faith and believe God from the get-go instead of waiting for 30 days and then having to start believing God!"

Ben said with a fun sarcasm, "That was like a window in which God, Himself, was probably going to freak out at Y2K for thirty days and might not be able to pull Himself together and handle it—for at least a month. We should definitely get beans and guns."

Tim nodded but the look on his face betrayed the fact that he was holding in a series of comedic comebacks.

Doug continued, "I told my friend it was kind of weird, saying 'If anyone has material possessions and sees his brother in need but has no pity on him, how can the love of God be in him?' So if you store up for thirty days, but I haven't stored up for thirty days and I have needs...then you have to help me out of your supply!'"

Ben laughed and said to Doug, "What a great attitude. If I knew you were a beans and guns guy, I could have just come to you on January 2nd, 2000 and said, 'Hey, look, I am going to need your help. You are now under a mandate to exercise selfless giving and I am going to need a bunch of your beans and one of your guns.'"

"I believe that if we are being motivated by fear it is not from the Father," said Doug. "The heart of the Father is to love us and encourage us into His purpose for us. And I believe that a lot of what has happened has been motivated out of fear. I remember in the 70's and the 80's and the 90's words would be given about Jesus' coming or something else, and people where caught up in them because of fear. And when it didn't happen people got mad at God. About every ten years or so people forget how dumb they are, so the devil brings another revelation to them and they get caught up in stupidity again."

"That reminds me about a website that I hear people quoting —this prophetic website," explained Ben, with a slight smile at the realization that he had just uttered the words 'prophetic website.'

"People go and read all of this stuff and everything they come back with is some apocalyptic hoo-ha that they are fearful about. At one point there was just so much fear about it that I told the people I knew who read it to quit. I said, 'Stop going to that website. You are not getting anything out of it. I know you think that the big cheese prophets are downloading the manna from heaven, but what you come out with is just a fear-sandwich. It makes me want to exclude you from my parties. Fear is no fun.'"

"There is going to be some persecution coming on the earth, but think about Joseph," Doug said. "God gave him revelation of what he had to do. So he stored up for seven years for the seven-year famine but he didn't do it out of fear. He did it out of the abundance of those seven years. He enjoyed the seven years that he was in, preparing at the same time for the next seven years. So, I am not against preparing when God speaks something to you but you don't do it out of fear," summarized Doug.

"Joseph didn't say to bring everything you have. He told the people to bring the excess in because they were going to need it in another seven years. So there was still a peace in that seven years of preparation and it wasn't motivated by fear. It was motivated by obedience to what he had heard the Lord speak. Again, faith comes by hearing and hearing by the word."

Doug paused for a moment and then chuckled. "I remember Kenneth Hagen, of course he is dead now, but in 1974 or 1975 he told me this story. He said that he was with a man that graduated from Kenneth's school, and the man was sharing that God had spoken to him, saying to give his car to a particular missionary. Well, the man gave his car to this missionary and in just a couple of days someone came up and gave him a brand-new Cadillac.

"All of the students heard this and were excited. They knew this man had heard the Lord and he gave away his car and that God then replaced it with a brand new car. Hagan said 'you know what was interesting? For the next six months I had a lot of students walking.'"

Ben and Tim chuckled too, glad that Doug took the time to tell the story.

"It's one thing hearing from the Father but it is another thing trying to get in on what the Father has done for someone else," Doug explained. "Some students gave away their cars because they thought they were going to get a Cadillac, too. But they didn't hear the Father tell them that. They heard the testimony of how God blessed someone else's obedience. But if we just assume that 'if God did it for you then He will do it for me,' we might be walking for six months."

Ben leaned forward and noted, "That is a perfect example of not walking as a son who is aware of the Father's love and being confident that He can talk to you. You hear a word of truth like that, an experience that was real. You convert it into a formula if you're in the mentality of a slave. But you don't need to convert it into a formula if you are a son, because you are already fully aware that the Father loves you and you have your own personal trusting relationship with Him."

Doug sat back. "But when we exercise faith in what we hear the Father say, then the Father obligates Himself to respond.

However, what you treasure reveals your heart. What was in their hearts was that they would look good in a Cadillac. You need to be careful that your identity is not in what you have, but in who you are in Christ."

"This must have been in the 70's. I am not sure if any students now would look good driving a Cadillac. Maybe an Escalade," smiled Ben.

"That is good to know," Doug snapped back. "So if someone gives you a brand new Cadillac, Ben, you would just give it to me because you don't think you would look good in one."

Ben shrugged.

"In II Corinthians 5 it talks about how we walk by faith and not by sight. We don't walk by what we see, which are the temporal things. We walk by faith in eternal things. We walk by faith in what we hear the Lord speaking to our spirits, not by what we see with our natural eyes. A lot of times if I walk by what I see, I would be depressed and discouraged and never leave my home. But you can't go by what you see. You have to go by what you hear the Father speak. Abraham did that. It says that it was credited to him as righteousness because he acted on what he heard, not by what he saw.

"When we act on what we hear from the Lord and we don't pay attention to what we see, what we see ends up being transformed into what we have heard.

"In Galatians it says, 'now the life I live in the flesh, I live by faith...' I live by that which I hear the Father speaking to me. I hear that which the Son of God has revealed to me and accomplished for me, and I believe that everything God requires of me Christ has already finished for me."

Tim reflected back to Doug: "You take hold of it by your faith in Him, and in doing so give evidence to what's not seen."

Ben spoke up too, "When we talk about having a heavenly mindset, it seems to me that Jesus set that example for us because He showed us how the Son lives in peace. The disciples would be all worried, 'How did you do this?' And He would just tell them that He was doing what He saw the Father doing and He was saying what He heard the Father saying. I wonder if that is an example of how we learn to get a heavenly mindset. To have faith in those things that are eternal.

"That seems to be what you are saying when you talk about listening to what the Father is saying and tuning into your relationship with Him. You can apply that connection to the things that are all around you in the natural. People wonder what you are doing. I guess that is how you can explain it."

"I think that is true," affirmed Doug. "I have a son. When he got old enough to mow the grass, I would tell him to go mow the grass. Well, he had liberty to go mow the grass the way he wanted to, but he heard my voice say go mow the grass and he got to exercise faith and mow the grass how he wanted. I might mow the grass straight forward and backwards but he might mow the grass in circles or whatever. I think God gives us options when we hear the voice of the Lord to go do something. We are to do that according to the grace that He has given us and our giftings. And that is how we can fulfill what we have heard the Father speak."

"By being ourselves," added Tim.

Doug hummed in approval and said, "I can hear the Father say something and it might look completely different than what you have heard the Father saying to you because our giftings and our graces are different. But we have both accomplished what the Father has told us to do. That is why the word talks about it being foolishness to compare ourselves with one another because our graces are different and our giftings are different. So it is not in how we do it; it is in doing it."

"I bet a lot of people are going to say, "Well, I know that Jesus said He could hear the Father, but that is because He was Jesus. How can you say we can hear the Lord?" Ben pondered. "I know some Christians that will even get angry if you say that you heard the Father tell you to do this or do that. That makes them feel diminished because they feel like they don't have the same radio receiver that you have and they get under condemnation because of it. Can I hear the Lord, too?" he asked, assuming their position.

Tim understood where Ben was coming from and added, "There are plenty of people that would equate the language of 'hearing the Lord' into just knowing what the Scriptures say or exercising sound moral reasoning, but that is not what you are talking about is it?"

"I can give you several examples," Doug said. "God speaks to us in many avenues. He speaks to us through His word. He speaks to us through circumstances. He speaks to us through revelation by His Spirit. He can speak to us though other people.

"When I was ministering in Georgia a few years ago I was taking a shuttle bus to the airport and as I got off the shuttle bus, the shuttle bus driver turned to me and told me I might consider buying such-and-such a stock. Well, I thought that was strange. Later, I talked to my wife and I said 'you know I think the Lord was speaking to me through this.' I went online and did some research on that stock and invested in it and had a 49% return on that stock! Now, I believe that God spoke to me through that shuttle bus driver in order to bless me with finances to do the things He has called me to do. So he who has ears, let him hear what the Spirit of the Lord is speaking. We try to make it so mystical and religious that we sometimes miss the simplicity of God speaking.

"The word says, 'pray without ceasing.' I think part of praying without ceasing is quieting our spirit to listen to God speaking. It is not all in what we say; it is in listening to what He is speaking. We can have this attitude when we are fishing or playing golf or driving down the road. Our spirit can always be sensitive to what the Spirit of the Lord is speaking to us. When we ask the Lord to give to us out of what we have already heard Him say, we are then asking out of who He is, not out of the needs we have."

"Do you think every believer can hear God?" asked Ben.

"I believe that every person has the ability to hear the Lord. The problem is we have got to humble ourselves and understand the simplicity of His speaking," replied Doug. "I believe that everyone has a seed of faith. But a seed is expected to grow and mature and produce. Levels of faith are mentioned throughout the word—no faith, little faith, lack of faith, weak faith, full of faith, great faith. As we agree with all the Father speaks, we will continue to understand the authority given to us as His sons.

"God spoke to me once just saying, 'Hey, I love you.' Well, that changed my whole world. It is not the amount of words He speaks. It is not the quantity; it is the quality. We get so caught up in so many words and we can't hear the Lord speak because we are begging Him. We have that beggar mentality—we do not understand the authority He has given us as sons. We have to come asking the Lord, asking the Lord, asking the Lord. One time I felt like the Lord said, 'Well, if you would quit asking and just listen, I have the answer for you. I have already given you provision; all you need to do is appropriate it.' I think a lot of times God is speaking but we are just not listening."

Doug continued with sincerity, "I would encourage people just to pray 'well, Lord, I want to quiet myself.' The word says, 'Be still and know that I am God.' There is a time to be still and meditate in the presence of the Lord.

"I said 'meditate' and now people are going to think we are going into the new age and all that stuff. But you know, before the new age was, God was. And God said, 'Be still and know.' I think the devil always tries to corrupt what the purpose of God is. Meditation is not an evil thing if you are being quiet before the Lord. I think it is just quieting our spirit, quieting our soul, so that we can be attentive to what He is saying."

Ben followed up his original question: "Some people would ask 'How do I know if it is the Lord?' That, of course, is the next question right after, 'Can I hear God?'

Doug said, "I think as you grow in the Lord and in your ability to hear the Lord, your faith is going to rise. But at the very beginning, a very good way to know whether it is the Lord is to remember that God is never going to contradict His word. So when you hear the Lord speaking to you, if you can't confirm it in the written word then I would question if God really spoke it to you. God is not limited to the written words of the Bible, but He does confirm His word."

Ben, satisfied with that answer leaned back and said, "That is very particular. That is common advice for those that struggle about whether the Lord is still speaking. You need to know the word of God. If you don't know who He is and how He acts, what He has said in the past and what His manner is, it would be hard to discern. He is not going to change His manner or change His direction."

"That is why it says in Psalm 119 to hide the word of God in your heart so you won't sin. When we have the word in our heart, then when we hear these other voices, we can say, 'Hey that is contrary to the word. That is contrary to the nature of the Father. So I don't believe that is the Lord,'" explained Doug.

"Also, when God is speaking to you He will bring confirmation. I don't know how many times God has spoken to me in an area and then I will get home and my wife will say something out of the blue to confirm it. In II Corinthians 13 it says, 'out of the mouth of two or three let a thing be established.' God wants us to grow and mature, so if God is speaking to us, He is going to confirm it. We just have to step out.

"A lot of people use 'fleeces' to try to get confirmation, and I think when you're younger in your faith and in your walk, God will honor that. But there comes a time where God says you need to go on now from the elementary things and begin to walk as a son in the understanding of what He has called you to be. That is exercising faith.

"It is just like in the natural. We are all born with muscles but people that work out with weights develop their muscles more than people that don't work out. God has given each one of us a measure of faith, but sometimes our faith is not as active as other people's because we are not exercising it. The Scripture talks about being an overcomer. How can you be an overcomer if you never have to overcome anything? We will talk more about that later.

"I want to switch gears right now and talk about faith in action."

Doug spent a few seconds reviewing some Scriptures in his notes, took a deep breath, and then continued.

"In all of the stories that are written about people exercising faith and miracles happening, they consistently believed in who He is. I believe that God has given each of us faith to exercise. There are several accounts of the faith of various people in the

Bible, and sometimes miracles are done according to the faith of one, while other times it is when two or three come into agreement that miracles occur. Sometimes it might be a brother's faith that allows me to come into something. There may be an area where I don't have faith to believe so God honors someone else's faith on my behalf.

"In Matthew 8, the story of the centurion who came imploring Jesus for the healing of his servant, the Lord says something remarkable: 'I have not found so much faith in all Israel.'

"What was special about this man's faith?"

Tim jumped in, "This was a man that understood authority. He said he told one person to go and he went; another to come and he came. He recognized the authority of Jesus."

Doug explained further. "He said he didn't deserve to have the Lord under his roof. He knew if Jesus would just speak the word then it would happen. This man didn't need the visitation or the laying on of hands. His hope was that Jesus would just send the word. He believed in who He was and the power of what He spoke."

"And so he received what Jesus had—a miracle of healing!" Tim said.

"In Matthew 9 Jesus healed blind men saying, 'according to your faith will it be done to you,'" said Doug.

"Interestingly, he had previously asked them if they believed in who he was when he asked, 'Do you believe that I am able to do this?'" Tim pointed out.

Doug nodded.

"A lot of times the testing that we go through is so that we will know. It is not that God is wanting to know if I have faith. It is so that I may know that I have faith. Once I believe for something and it happens, it is something that I have experienced. The next time, then, I am already confident that God is able to do that. It is not something I have to generate faith for, or something I have only read about. It is something I have experienced. You take a man with an experience—you can't take that experience from him. Now a man that just has an intellectual thought, someone more intellectual can out-argue him from what he thinks. But a man that has an experience—I don't care how smart you are—it's hard to change his mind about what he has experienced."

"That is brilliant on so many different levels," said Ben. "One of the things that I have noticed is that guys who have suffered and have come out the other side understanding a little bit more about how God is with them during suffering are the guys that I tend to want to trust faster than guys who talk a lot but haven't yet suffered."

"There are some things that I know about God that no one is going to take away from me and we will talk more about that in another chapter," said Doug, "but I know that God loves me. And I don't care what happens. You can't take away from me the knowing that God loves me because I know He does. God has proven Himself faithful time and time again. That is that foundation that we have.

"Now that is contrary to the natural mind. It is contrary to the religious system but it is the heart of the Father. Matthew 21 says, 'if you have faith and don't doubt.' What is having faith and not doubting? Faith is hearing the word of the Lord and then not doubting when you see what you see. A lot of times we hear the Lord and then we step out and then all of a sudden what we see is contrary to what we've heard so we start saying 'well, yeah, but this is what I see so this must be what is true' so we choose what we see instead of believing in what we have heard."

Ben added, "This seems to relate so perfectly now, going back to the very first foundation that you laid in this book—knowing that God loves you. If you don't trust His heart for you then when circumstances or what He's doing around you doesn't add up in your rational mind you might draw conclusions about Him that are not true."

"Most definitely," said Doug.

Ben continued, "But if you start with 'I trust in who He is' exclusively—without reservation—then the things around you don't spell for you different words and sentences about Him than what you know to be true. In the natural, my wife and I will occasionally run up into something where there is a conflict. Usually it starts with me saying something stupid. I have noticed in those moments that Robin has a choice. On one hand she could say to herself 'oh, I know your heart. That was just something stupid that you said' and she can forgive me and tell me I am being an idiot and it is all funny and over with. On the other hand, if she hears the stupid words that I say and concludes, 'his heart has changed toward me...he has stopped loving me,' then she has to go into all kinds of personal defense modes in order to survive. These places where we draw conclusions about each other based on some loose words or actions can really mess up a whole day!"

Doug added, "That's what starts divorce. That's what starts separation. That's what starts division. That doubt comes in about the other person. She thinks, 'Well, Ben really doesn't love me. So and so really doesn't appreciate me.' What does that produce? It opens a can of everything that is contrary to the word of God in the heart of the Father."

Ben thought for a moment. "As soon I bring a judgment in like that where I judge a situation and say 'she doesn't love me' or 'she doesn't this, that and the other,' I have immediately started building walls.

"We can do this with God, too," Ben continued, "if God doesn't act right. A lot of people lose their ability to trust God simply because God failed them in action or inaction at a time in their journey and they made a judgment against God. They say, 'That is who He is—a God who plays favorites on a whim. He might help you, Doug, but because He didn't help me then He doesn't really love me.' That's a judgment and we build walls between us and the Father and eventually it is hard to say, 'Okay, now I am going to trust Him.' It is so hard to get over that kind of disappointment and judgment."

"It is interesting that we just came back to the second foundation, which is forgiveness," observed Tim. "A lot of people don't know how to forgive God or recognize that they feel He didn't act right. We take up offenses in our heart because 'He didn't provide for me,' or 'He didn't come through,' or 'He didn't help me.' We have all kinds of complaints about God not acting like we thought He should have acted. We say, 'He didn't heal them,' or, 'He didn't do what He said.' That becomes a judgment and if we don't forgive God, it will keep us from having a trusting relationship with Him.

"That is a hard thing to begin to talk about because it seems to imply that God did something wrong," Tim went on. "I think a key to understanding what we're talking about here is this: we are not saying that God sinned. We are saying that a perceived offense is still an offense. So if it hurt my heart, I can still take up an offense that needs to be forgiven, even if God didn't do anything wrong. I think that is true with people too. You may have failed to meet my expectations in something but it doesn't mean that you necessarily sinned. You may have been hearing the Lord about something and acting in perfect obedience to Him, but if what you did hurt me I still have to forgive you for it because it is still an offense that I took into my heart."

"That is exactly right," said Ben.

"In James 1:2-8 it says, 'Consider it pure joy, my brothers, whenever you face trials of many kinds, because you know that the testing of your faith develops perseverance. Perseverance must finish its work so that you may be mature and complete, not lacking anything. If any of you lacks wisdom, he should ask God, who gives generously to all without finding fault, and it will be given to him. But when he asks, he must believe and not doubt, because he who doubts is like a wave of the sea, blown and tossed by the wind. That man should not think he will receive anything from the Lord; he is a double-minded man, unstable in all he does.'

"When I come into serious trial or tribulation, I know that it is a strengthening of my faith, not a weakening of my faith. I believe in who He is. My faith is not in my ability to do things. My faith is in God's ability to work through me to accomplish those things He has called me to do. I think people come short of the goal. They step out in faith and they believe God for this and believe God for that and then all of a sudden what they are believing for doesn't happen and then they say, 'Well God, you don't love me.' And the devil is right there saying, 'Yeah, you know this walking by faith deal is good for a believer that God loves but God doesn't love you so you might as well quit walking by faith and just trust in your flesh.' When you trust in your flesh you are not able to see the provision that God has for you."

Doug looked up and made eye contact with Tim and Ben. He continued.

"This journey we are on, it is not really about us. It is really about Him in us. I think that is part of the process of taking up your cross daily and denying yourself. It is a day-to-day walk of faith with God and with one another. Faith is not something we use every now and then. Faith is something that we live in. It is not something that I appropriate here and appropriate there. It is a daily walk of trusting in who He is.

"As it also says in James," affirmed Tim, "everything that does not come from faith is sin."

Doug agreed. "In Romans 4 it says God 'gives life to the dead and calls into being that which does not exist.' I have seen God time and time again in situations where I needed something to fulfill the purpose of what He has called me to do and I ask Him and all of a sudden things just start changing. And then all of a sudden it is taken care of."

"I like how you said that," said Tim. "It was to fulfill something that God had spoken to you and your faith was in who He is. Just reemphasizing, you were not distrusting in your capacity to believe for something that you needed but your faith had its origin in who God was and in what He spoke. I really think that points back to that first foundation that God loves you. If you really believe that He loves you, that you can really be connected to Him, and that your place in His heart is totally sure, then you can look at faith that way. It has its origin in something. If you don't really believe that God loves you in every part of your heart then it's easy to turn faith into a destination instead of the vehicle that gets you there."

Doug affirmed Tim's words and quoted John 15 saying, "'You did not choose, me but I chose you.' What does that say? I didn't choose Him. He chose me. So the foundation is that God loves me, and because He loves me, He chose me. He has chosen me and He has appointed me to go bear fruit—*fruit that will last.* It goes on to say, 'Then the Father will give you whatever you ask in my name.'

"What is Jesus saying here? God has chosen me. He loves me. He has called me to go and bear fruit. Now, whatever I need to bear the fruit that he has appointed me to bear, I just ask Him in Jesus' name and the Father will give it that He may be glorified.

"The question here is not the things that I need to make me look good but the things that I need to fulfill what He has called and appointed me to do. No matter what God has called me and appointed me to do in the ministry or in the business world or whatever, I can ask Him for what I need to fulfill that and He is going to give it to me because it glorifies Him. It doesn't glorify me. It glorifies Him. People have taken that concept and said, 'Well, Father, you said whatever I need or whatever I asked in Jesus' name you would give it to me,' but the key here is that we ask according to what He has appointed us to do."

Doug paused for the point to sink in.

"That other way doesn't have to do with something that the Father originally spoke or who He is," Tim pointed out again. "It is trying to apply the principle of faith without the foundation of God's love and purpose at the center of it."

Doug had a faint smile like he was revisiting a fond memory.

"There have been times over the years that the Lord said, 'I want to heal that person. Go pray for them.' And I would go pray for them and God would heal them. Or God would say to go do a certain thing and I would go do it and God would do what He said He'd do. There has never been a time when I acted on what I heard the Lord say when God didn't do what He said He would.

But there have been lots of times that I assumed that a person needed healing or that something else needed to be done when I would say: 'I am going to ask you Lord to do this thing because it would be a good thing if you did.' Sometimes God went ahead and did what I asked but a lot of times He didn't because it wasn't His purpose at that time; it was only my assumption.

"Sometimes it is hard to discern," admitted Ben, "and I have sympathy on those who are struggling with hearing and knowing and believing and seeing what God will do. I had a friend last year whose mom got terminally ill with cancer, and he really sensed that God said, 'I am going to heal your mom.' My friend didn't say, 'I think it is a good idea for my mom to be healed—I am going to ask God to heal my mom.' Nope, he said, 'Ben, I think I heard the Lord say that He is going to heal her.'

"So he prays for her and believes God, but she dies in a few months.

"This, for him, has been a very difficult time of crisis of understanding in hearing the Lord. Did the Lord do it right? Did He do it wrong? Where did it go wrong? These things can get out of hand in our hearts pretty fast."

"I would say that His mom is healed now," said Doug.

"Some would say that that is a little bit of an 'easy out' there, Doug. I understand what you are saying and I am with you but some people would look at that and just say, 'Really?'"

Without hesitation Doug said, "See, Ben, this is the simplicity of my faith. I hear the Lord speak things and sometimes I filter that through my understanding of what I think He said when, really, my filter might need to be changed. If I think I heard the Lord say something and things don't seem to line up, then I just say, 'Well, Lord you didn't do anything bad here, I just didn't have the full understanding.' That is why it says you need to ask for wisdom."

He continued, "Now the devil can use that and attack and steal that man's destiny because of that one thing. Because the devil says, 'You didn't really hear God because look what happened. God doesn't love you; He won't speak to you.' So if you're in that situation you have to rule that thought. You have to rule that emotion. You have to say, 'I heard the Lord. I just misunderstood and misapplied what I heard Him say.' That is an act of our believing in who He is, not in what we see. Now is it fun? No. Is it easy? No. But it is foundational because the devil is going to use everything he can to rob us of our destiny. So in situations like that, we have got to be like David and say, 'Soul, bless the Lord.' It is a choice. That is why it says we need to take every thought captive. We have to rule our minds. And we don't allow the enemy to come in and sow that doubt that would rob us of our destiny and the future of what God has for us to do."

Doug put his hand down on the notebook lying on the couch beside him.

"Now that might sound hard and cold but it is truth and reality. There have been a lot of times in my life that I have suffered loss. I had one guy tell me one time, 'You have lost so much stuff. Why are you still serving God?'

"I asked him, 'What does stuff have to do with serving God?'

"He said, 'There is a lot of people that have quit serving God just because of what they felt like God didn't do for them. And here all this stuff you have been through, and you still believe in God?'

"I said, 'Well, I question if they ever knew the Father.' I have been forgiven so much. I deserved hell and God's love saved me and God has already done so much for me that if He never does anything else, He's worthy of my praise and love for the rest of my life. Even if He never says another thing or never does another deed. What He's done is already enough but because He is God and because of His character and His nature and His love He is going to continue doing amazing things, but I don't serve God for what I get out of it. I serve God for who He is.

"When I say things like, 'Well, God you let me down in this deal.' Who is that really about? It is all about me. We need to realize that because of what He has already done He deserves our praise and love for the rest of our life. That is coming into sonship. That is coming into the foundation of God's love. It is not, 'Well, God if you love me, do this. If you love me do that.' It is, 'God you are God and I love you. And because I love you, I want to be with you. I want to have a relationship with you because of what you have done already.'"

"Mmmmm," Ben murmured.

Doug didn't slow down: "So it is a foundation issue and a trust issue. We can't let the enemy come in and rob us of our sonship and identity. Our hurts get blown out of proportion and we question everything we've ever believed when we could simply say, 'Hey, I probably missed God or misinterpreted what God spoke.'"

"Because," Ben interjected, "if you know that God loves you and you know that He is love and not that He just acts loving, then that challenges us to trust Him at all times. I think the cross wins our hearts because it shows us for the first time how God really feels about us. That's why the cross is where people have to make a decision about God. And that decision is not really 'do I believe that God died on the cross to save me?' It's not really that cold. It is more, 'do I really believe God loves me that much?' Because if you can believe He loves you that much and you can receive it, then salvation enters in and your whole life and your understanding of who you are changes. It is not just believing that He died on a cross in an economic sin exchange. I am not sure if that means anything by itself. But do you believe He loves you that much?"

"If you do, you have to change your view of yourself to someone who is beloved. That's a total shift," added Tim.

"I think that is why I John says, 'This is the victory that has overcome the world, our faith.' Our faith in what? Our faith in believing that He loves us that much. Our faith in believing He paid the price for us. This is the victory that has overcome the world. Our faith in believing who He is," Doug said with a tone of completion.

He looked through the window at the last glowing embers of the campfire for a moment.

"I want to shift gears a little bit here. In Ephesians it talks about putting on the full armor of God. In verse 16, it says, 'In addition to all this, take up the shield of faith, with which you can extinguish all the flaming arrows of the evil one.' Part of what your friend is going through is those flaming arrows that the enemy is shooting at him. The shield of faith protects us from those flaming arrows. What are some flaming arrows? The first arrow that the devil ever shot was when the serpent asked Eve, 'Has God said?'

Flaming arrows always question God's truth. Has God really saved us? Do all of these things really work for good for those that love God and are called according to His purpose? Will God really provide for me in my greatest need? Does God really forgive my sin? Can God really cleanse me from all unrighteousness? Does God really love me? Can God really relieve the pain in my heart? Does God really heal? Can God really take this disease from me? You can just go on and on."

"Those are all the flaming arrows," said Ben.

In affirmation Doug continued, "Each one of us has different flaming arrows being fired at us. An arrow is an accusation that the devil brings, challenging what we have heard the Lord speak to us. That shield of faith is our protection against those flaming arrows. But when we are not walking in the full armor of God and exercising faith, and when those flaming arrows come to attack our mind, then those thoughts poison our mind and we begin to believe the lie, saying 'God really doesn't love me.' Well, that shield of faith is part of our armor to guard our minds from the accusations the devil uses to try and discredit what the Father has spoken.

"If faith comes by hearing, I believe that if we start hearing the lie of the enemy, we can exercise negative faith to agree with the devil, and that is going to contradict true faith in what God has spoken. A lot of people are walking in the lie of what the enemy has spoken and are exercising faith in that. They are agreeing with the lie instead of agreeing with the truth.

"It says 'if two of you on earth agree about anything...' So, who are you agreeing with? What have you come into agreement with? Are you coming into agreement with that which you have heard from the Father or are you coming into agreement with that which you have heard from the devil? Both are powerful. If I come into agreement that I am a failure, that I never will obtain anything, that I'm always going to be disappointed, and that I am always going to be hurt, then what happens?

Let's say I enter into a relationship believing 'well, I am going to be hurt in this relationship because I always get hurt in a relationship.' What happens then is that I end up getting hurt in relationship. Why? Because I've agreed with the lie. That is why I think it's important to have the shield of faith and that armor of God to extinguish the accusations that contradict a revelation in the word of God that He has spoken to you. That is a foundation that we have to have."

Tim was listening and deep in thought, also watching the embers. He returned his gaze to his friends in the RV and said, "So if by faith we call things into being that the Lord has spoken before they really are, like we mentioned in Romans 4 where it says, 'The Lord calls things that aren't as though they were,' there is also a way that we can exercise that to our harm. There is a verse, I am not sure where it is right now, but it says 'as a man thinks, so is he.'"

Ben agreed, "There is a certain sense in which we can exercise our authority, but not for good, because what we say and what we believe is so powerful sometimes we can believe ourselves into less than what the Father is speaking because we aren't able to raise our vision. I have learned from personal experience that if you believe even a subtle lie, you can plant that lie around you and invite other people into your negative faith. You can create a relational environment by which other people get trapped in your misbeliefs about yourself or your poor beliefs about God just because you believe something stupid that the enemy came and whispered to you years ago. It doesn't just affect you and your relationship with God; it creates dysfunction and a pathology or a mental brokenness that can affect everybody around you.

"And this is why," he said, "coming into our sonship—which means really believing that God loves us that much—begins to help us break and take authority over thoughts that disagree with God's love. Break thoughts that bring accusations against Him. And it really changes our whole atmosphere. It changes the world.

It changes our families. It changes our kids. It changes our wives. When we start believing the truth about God's love for us and breaking down all of the stupid ideas, it changes everything."

"That is the key," said Doug. "If our faith is never tested, it can never be proven. I believe that God is looking for proven faith. We take Him at His word and we say 'Father I believe you and therefore I am going to take action on it' and it becomes a proven faith. We take God's word as reality and it becomes not something that we hear but something that we are. It is different for each one of us when the enemy comes and shoots flaming arrows, but once we overcome one lie or temptation and we prove in our own minds that our faith has superseded our natural eyes, then the devil doesn't tempt us there any longer.

"I remember when I first got saved," reminisced Doug. "I did a lot of drugs and stuff. God just delivered me from a lot of those habits, but I still smoked some marijuana. Here I was loving the Lord, baptized in the Holy Ghost, speaking in tongues, but still smoked a little pot. One day, the Lord confronted me and told me that it was sin. I thought, 'Man, I didn't know that was sin.' I really didn't know. That was how ignorant I was. I really didn't know! I didn't have the word in my heart. And anyway there wasn't any place that I read in the Scripture where it said 'Thou shall not smoke marijuana.' But when God convicted me that that was sin, I repented and God delivered me. Well, sometime in the next day or two I went to a place where some of my old friends were and I walked in and there was just a lot of marijuana on the table."

"And you just made a hand motion that made it look like a large Thanksgiving turkey," said Ben for the benefit of those not present to see Doug's gesture.

Doug laughed, "The dining room table had a couple pounds of pot that had just been opened up and it was just laying there and people were just going up there, rolling their joints and smoking. When I walked into the place, I didn't know that was happening. When they saw me they said, 'Hey, Doug good to see you.' These were people that I had smoked dope with, sold dope to, and hung out with when I was in my worldly ways. 'Try this,' they said.

"I looked at it and I said, 'No, I don't need that. God has set me free from that.'

"Then they said, 'Man, what are you on?' They thought I was on some high that they didn't know about yet.

"I just shared. 'I got saved. I got born again and baptized in the Holy Ghost and I don't need that anymore.' And I have never been tempted since that day to do drugs again. It has been thirty-four years."

Doug smiled and continued.

"See, God convicted me of something and I saw it as sin. I repented of it and I asked God to forgive me, but then the devil immediately came and tempted me in what God had released me from. But after I appropriated what God had spoken to me and said I didn't need it anymore, the devil has never tempted me in that area again. Why? Because he knows that marijuana is not a temptation to me.

"Now, he might tempt me in other things that I am still battling with, but he doesn't tempt me in that particular area because I have victory in that area. I have exercised faith believing in what God has spoken to me.

"It is that simple. The biggest problem we have is when we try to make it too complicated. We try to make faith and other things so difficult that we never can attain them, so we miss the blessing of what we already have in Christ.

"I believe that this will help people to exercise faith. The first part is believing that He is, and then knowing He is a rewarder of those that seek Him. Know that He was the one that first loved you."

FOUNDATION NUMBER FOUR:
KNOWING THE HOLY SPIRIT

"Well good mornin'," said Doug cheerily.

Tim got out of his truck, rubbed his cold hands together and took in the sunrise. He pulled a chair up close to the small fire that was already crackling and popping. "Mornin'," he repeated groggily. As Tim shuffled around the campfire he thought to himself, 'I have never been awake before Doug, and he has a mood at six in the morning that I can't find until after breakfast and two cups of coffee. How does he do it?'

"Has Laurie had that baby yet?" Doug said, interrupting Tim's thoughts.

"You think if she did I'd be in the woods with men?" Tim chided. "No, but any time now." Tim had driven down the mountain after last night's recording was finished in order to sleep at home with his wife, who was due to have their second baby right at the end of the camp-out.

"She must really think a lot of you to let you spend your days fishing, hiking, and hanging out with guys while she's pregnant and has a two-year-old running around the house. Or maybe she just wants to get rid of you," he smiled.

"Or she knows your book won't be any good without me," Tim shot back slyly despite his sleepiness.

Ben stepped out of the RV with scrambled eggs and some large strips of bacon and presented them to Tim and Doug.

"Thanks, I'm so hungry," said Tim, who started eating without any hesitation whatsoever.

Ben followed with fresh cups of coffee, which Tim held on to like a man lost in the ocean clings to a raft.

Breakfast was quiet except for talk of afternoon showers in the forecast, the dreaming-up of canoeing and fishing plans for the evening, and the comforting crackle of the campfire. Beams of sun came over the treetops and changed the landscape. As the embers cooled from orange to gray, the three men leaned back in their chairs and felt the warmth on their faces.

"All fueled up?" asked Ben. They threw their paper plates in the fire and hopped into the RV, ready to record another discussion.

Doug fired away, "I am going to talk about the most controversial gift that the Father has given us. The devil despises and hates it so much. And the spirit of religion really doesn't like it much either.

"It is the promise of the Holy Spirit.

"The Holy Spirit is one of the gifts that the Father Himself has given us as a promise to ensure our inheritance. John the Baptist was a forerunner of Jesus and he says, 'I baptize you with water. But one more powerful than I will come, the thongs of whose sandals I am not worthy to untie. He will baptize you with the Holy Spirit and with fire.'

"I believe that the Bible is plain about the salvation experience and the baptism of the Holy Spirit. I believe you need to receive both. As for myself, when I pray for people to receive Jesus as their Savior, I then lead them in a prayer to receive the baptism of the Holy Spirit. Because that is the best time to receive it, before they have any religious tradition that tells them that they don't need the Holy Spirit or that the Holy Spirit is not for today."

"I remember back in 1974," Doug chuckled almost imperceptibly as he continued, "after I got saved, I received the baptism of the Holy Spirit. I was attending a Baptist fellowship at the time. The pastor called me in and said, 'Doug, I want to talk to you. You are really having a salvation experience. Man, you are on fire for the Lord. I recognize that in you but I need to talk to you. I need to warn you about this Holy Spirit stuff and speaking in tongues. That is not for today. That has been done away with.' I said, 'Well, Pastor, it is too late. I have already received Him. If you had told me that before I did then I might have bought into what you're saying, but I have already got Him. It is too late.' The funny part about it now is that that man has received the baptism of the Holy Spirit—it is too late for him, as well."

Doug was now reminiscing more than teaching. "I had other people tell me that speaking in tongues was of the devil; I told them, 'When I was in a world of sin, I never heard anyone speak in tongues. It wasn't until I started hanging out with believers that I heard people speaking in tongues. So I would have to disagree with what you are telling me because if tongues were of the devil, I would have heard it years ago when I was hanging out with sinners.'

"To me the promise of the Father—the Holy Spirit—is a vital foundation that we have to have in our lives because He empowers us and gives us gifts and brings to remembrance what Jesus has done for us. I think one reason the Holy Spirit is so controversial in the Church today is that the devil doesn't want us to have Him, the promise of the Father, so he does everything he can to stop Him.

"Jesus even told His disciples in John 14:16-18, 'And I will ask the Father, and He will give you another Counselor to be with you forever—the Spirit of truth. The world cannot accept Him, because it neither sees Him nor knows Him. But you know Him, for He lives with you and will be in you. I will not leave you as orphans; I will come to you.'"

Ben made a brief observation: "He was foreshadowing Paul's statements in Romans 8 that it is by the Holy Spirit that we will cry out, 'Daddy, Father!'"

"Yes!" Doug didn't miss a beat, "One sign that guarantees us that we are not orphans is the Holy Spirit. But the devil wants us to be orphan-minded instead of son-minded. If he can keep us from receiving the Holy Spirit, we will be trapped in an orphan mentality. We will never think we are good enough for the things the Father has for us. Part of the blessing of the Holy Spirit is to take that orphan mentality away from us and reveal to us what the Father has for us in Christ."

"An orphan is obviously a child who doesn't know who his parents are," said Ben. "He has a sense of loss, of being disconnected, not quite being at home. And then Jesus sends the Holy Spirit, and, whatever else the Holy Spirit might do, He certainly convinces us that we have a home in the Father's love and He teaches us how to act like sons!"

Doug agreed, "When Jesus was baptized in the water by John, it said the Holy Spirit descended on Him like a dove. If the Holy Spirit descended on Jesus as a dove, it was an infilling of Jesus with the Holy Spirit in His earthly ministry. If Jesus needed the Holy Spirit to fulfill His purpose on the earth, we most surely need the Holy Spirit. At the ascension, Jesus tells us 'I have to go because if I don't go I can't send you the promise of the Father—the Holy Spirit.'"

Ben jumped in again, "As soon as the Holy Spirit descends, the next thing that happens is that a voice speaks from heaven and says, 'This is my son.' Again, the Holy Spirit comes and the proclamations of sonship and the Father's love are made full."

"That alone would keep the devil from wanting us to receive the Holy Spirit because the Holy Spirit brings us into a furthering of our identity," said Doug. "Luke 11 says, 'If you then, though you are evil, know how to give good gifts to your children, how much more will your Father in heaven give the Holy Spirit to those who ask Him!' The Holy Spirit is the gift of the Father for us."

"If the Holy Spirit is a gift of the Father," remarked Tim, "then He is pretty important for us to have. If the Father Himself says to you, 'I want to give you this,' why would we want to refuse Him? The Spirit must be important. Why wouldn't He want us to have Him? And why wouldn't we want to ask for Him?"

Ben grunted in solidarity with Tim.

Doug nodded, "It says in Acts 1, 'But you will receive power when the Holy Spirit comes on you; and you will be my witnesses in Jerusalem, and in all Judea and Samaria, and to the ends of the earth.' I think people have a lot of problems being the expression of Christ on the earth because they haven't received the power of the Holy Spirit to be His witnesses.

"But here is what we have been doing: We go to a building that we call *the Church* on Sunday and Wednesday nights and we think that is the place where we have to be to do what God has called us to, but that is not the truth. The truth is that everyday is the day that the Lord has made. And we are to be the Church wherever we are, expecting Him to be in our midst just because we're gathered together.

'It says we shall receive power to be His witnesses. Every place we go, we should be a witness of the demonstration of the power of God in the world, establishing His kingdom. You could describe the power of the Spirit like this: 'you shall have power here in Woodland Park, and then in the whole state of Colorado, and then in the United States, and then in the uttermost parts of the world. Wherever you live, that is the place that you shall receive power to be my witness.'"

"I am hearing you talk," Ben said as he let loose a laugh. "When you talk about power, I can't help it…I think about power tools. I like going to the garage and working with woodworking stuff—power tools. I will go to somebody's wood shop and if they have a really nice drill press or something that is awesome, and I will feel a little deficient as a wood worker," Ben smiled. "I think that is the same jealous spirit that gets on people when we talk about the power of the Holy Spirit or receiving the baptism in the Holy Spirit."

He paused and glanced at Doug and Tim, then continued his thought: "A lot of us have grown up in religions and in cultures that have taught us that you received everything you need when you got saved. You don't need anything else and when we hear something like, 'You need to receive the power of the Holy Spirit so you can do the work of evangelism better' it can generate something in us that feels like jealousy because we are thinking like orphans. We are going to compare our stuff to your stuff—your stuff to my stuff—and it immediately brings jealousy. That jealousy makes us feel awkward and deficient, so we put Him down. And by "Him" I mean the Holy Spirit.

"I think some people spiritual-warfare themselves right out of the Holy Spirit because they are convicted of jealousy and of feeling deficient when they first are told they need to receive the baptism. I wish we could defeat that. I think it tracks back to one thing and that is the first section of this book: we have to know that God is not a God of formulas, loopholes, contracts, amendments and constitutions, but He is the God who loves us! So we can look at the promise of the Holy Spirit and say, 'Thanks, Dad. I appreciate that gift. Thank you very much' and just enjoy Him. But if there is anything about understanding God's love that is not complete in us, then being told that we need to receive the baptism of Holy Spirit will set us into a jealous funk. It can take us off into mental delirium faster than most anything else I can think of."

Doug was right with Ben, "And who is right there to whisper in your ear that you are right in your justification? It is the devil. The devil doesn't want us to have the fullness that you are talking about.

"Now let's talk about some of the benefits of the Holy Spirit," Doug said.

"What is the work of the Holy Spirit that God gives us? One thing that the Holy Spirit gives us is power. Power to do what? Power to do what God has called us to do in Christ. The first time I met Tim and Laurie they were talking about wanting to be missionaries and I told them, 'Well have you received the baptism of the Holy Ghost yet?' And they said 'I don't know.' I told them, 'You don't need to go out and be a missionary if you haven't got the power to do what God sends you there to do. The devil will just eat up on you.' They weren't sure about the truth of that because of the traditions they had come from, but they have both received the Holy Spirit since then and have done great work in the kingdom."

Ben turned to Tim. "Was that hard to hear at first, Tim?"

Tim thought about it for a second and then answered, "My personal experience with the Lord was much more of a gradual process than Laurie's. I haven't had as clear or specific a blockage in my relationship with the Holy Spirit as Laurie did. I just needed to come into a fuller understanding and a fuller experience.

"For Laurie, it was harder for her to hear because of wounds she had. In the past, people who were filled with the Holy Spirit offended her by telling her that she was deficient and ineffective if she didn't speak in tongues, and she dealt with that 'insufficient woodworker' thing that you were talking about, Ben. She had to deal with it in prayer and overcome it, and that is what we did that day when we were together—within forty-five minutes of meeting Doug and Rita. Once she got rid of the judgments and the hurt that she had, she could receive the Holy Spirit and, of course, everything exploded into wonder from there."

Doug remembered Tim and Laurie's story, and spoke as though he was answering a question someone had asked him: "Some people teach that if you don't have the Holy Spirit you aren't even saved. That is not the truth. And some people say that if you don't speak in tongues that you are not saved and filled with the Holy Ghost. That's not true, either.

"I think about all the junk religion tries to sell, like 'We are better than you because we have the Holy Spirit. We are better than you because we speak in tongues.' I say, 'Well, if you are better than I am, then you ought to have more love for me. If getting the baptism in the Holy Spirit and speaking in tongues is going to make you more like God, then you ought to be more loving than you are.'

"Some people have a spirit of religion on them and they become so legalistic, even though they know the Holy Spirit, that they preach condemnation to us instead of preaching love. The more I spend time with the Father, the more I should express the Father's love to others. The Father is not a condemning, judging, full-of- accusation type person and so when we receive His Spirit we should be full of His character."

"Wow. To take that in the natural," Tim reflected, "if someone tells me I have my dad's spirit about me, they are saying I have the style, character, and presence of my dad. So if the Holy Spirit is the promise of the Father, receiving His Spirit should not make us lose touch with all the things that we love about the Father, or Jesus for that matter. On the contrary, the Spirit covers us with His style, character, and presence.

"How do you respond to people who have that sort of mentality about the Holy Spirit, Doug? You know, people who are quick to predict that if you keep going down the Holy Spirit track soon you will be putting snakes around your neck and acting loony?" Tim asked with a smirk.

"Well," said Doug plainly, "the Scripture they base that on is 'And these signs will accompany those who believe: In my name they will drive out demons; they will speak in new tongues; they will pick up snakes with their hands; and when they drink deadly poison, it will not hurt them at all; they will place their hands on sick people, and they will get well.' They have made this whole thing about needing to show that you have faith by handling snakes and proving they won't bite you and that you can drink poison and it won't hurt you."

"So there again we see the formula," Tim pointed out.

"I believe what the word is really telling us is that when we are doing the work that the Father has called us to do, no weapon formed against us will prosper. We don't have to walk in fear that something bad might happen," said Doug. "That is different than setting out to tempt and challenge God. That is what the devil tried to do with Jesus when he led Him into the wilderness. He tried to tempt Jesus to challenge God: 'If you are the Son of God, tell these stones to become bread.' But Jesus didn't give the devil an opportunity to be His judge. He just told him what the word said.

"And part of that was 'Do not put the Lord your God to the test,'" added Tim.

"We don't test what we know to be true," said Ben. "We only test what we are not sure of."

"When we get in the mindset that we have to prove *we are something* then we have missed it," summarized Doug.

"Isn't that a little bit of how a person who is an orphan in their soul interacts with an amazing story like that one?" asked Tim. "Instead of knowing and believing that we are rooted in God's love and His special provision for our lives, the orphan creates another formula saying, 'Look, we have to attempt this and see if it is true.' The orphan tries to make it into some sort of action or test to have confidence in."

Ben leaned in with a look of compassion on his face. "I am considering the person who is looking in on this conversation and thinking, 'maybe these guys are just easing me into it. Maybe this is all going to get crazy in another chapter or two.' They may also be thinking, 'I wonder if all that they are talking about is really for me.'

"Now if we are confident in the Father's love then we say, 'Of course it is for me! I have received the gift of the Holy Spirit in Jesus' name,' and we just walk in that gift. We don't have to fall over and speak in tongues. We don't really have to do anything. We just have to know we are believing and receiving. I received the Holy Spirit this morning and I will receive Him again tomorrow morning. Pray for me to receive the Holy Spirit more and more," asked Ben earnestly, nearly forgetting he was making a point.

"However," Ben refocused, "the orphan looks at this privilege and says, "Oh, no, this could be a 'pass or fail' moment in my journey with God." Receiving the Holy Spirit and His gifts become a test for this person. But since we know God does not test us like that to condemn us, we can reject that whole proposition as illegitimate."

"Once again we go back to the number one foundation of knowing God's love," observed Doug. "It is amazing how if you are not confident in the love of the Father, your whole journey is affected."

Ben had more: "There are others who have tried to throw out this whole conversation based on people they have seen who got involved in 'receiving the Holy Spirit' and became nutty. They based a judgment against the baptism of the Holy Spirit on meeting one looney-toon; it was all the proof they needed to get out of dodge.

"Here is the better rationale: If God is Father, Son and Holy Spirit and we know that the Father's character is love...and His Son came and demonstrated that love...then why would we expect the Holy Spirit to demonstrate any other spirit? He acts according to the values that have already been established by the Father and Son. Why would we expect Him to go squirreling off into weird-land after we receive Him?

"We should not.

"We should trust Him because it only makes sense to trust Him," Ben leaned back again as he finished his thought.

"It comes from judgments," Doug explained. "In Laurie's case, she had a hunger to seek the Lord, a hunger to know the Father and all that God had for her. But then she gets to a place where immature kids tried to push something down her throat and make her speak in tongues, condemning her if she did not. And then she made a judgment against herself, that she was not part of the 'Holy Spirit Club,' and against the Father, that He was holding out on her. What these kids should have done was just love Laurie in the midst of her journey and let the Holy Spirit do His own work.

"I think loving someone in the midst of his or her journey just comes freely to us. God does not force us to do anything. He paid the price for everything that He has for us to do but yet He does not make us get saved. It is a free choice. Salvation is a free gift that you can choose not to take. It is the same with receiving the gift of the Holy Spirit.

"Speaking in tongues is the perfect illustration of this. People ask me, 'When I receive the Holy Spirit do I have to speak in tongues?' Well, I say to them, 'You don't have to...but why wouldn't you?' It is like if I give you a new car and you took it but you didn't want the keys so you could drive it."

Laughing, Ben kept at Doug's analogy. "The thinking is that if I drove it I would run over a small child in the first two hours."

"I feel it is so silly, the way the Holy Spirit's character has been maligned by the weird things that man has done in His name, and the way men have dishonored the Holy Spirit in their fervor to share Him without first being rooted in some of the results and benefits of the Spirit, like love, peace, and receiving the adoption as sons," said Tim. "But if you believe what the Scriptures say about the Holy Spirit, then of course you want the Holy Spirit. There is nothing that you wouldn't want.

"In certain cases that name has been misused and abused, just like people have done a lot of terrible things in the name of Jesus, or like people have abused food. But we don't respond by stopping our belief in Jesus. And we don't give up food because it has been abused. We model what it means to honor the name of Jesus by living in His love. We enjoy food in a healthy way. So knowing the character of the Holy Spirit and the wonderful things the Scripture says about Him, we should respond to abuses and misrepresentations not by jettisoning the Holy Spirit altogether, but by having good, healthy relationships with the Holy Spirit."

"That is a very valid point," said Doug. "Every good gift the Father has for us, the enemy tries to counterfeit and pervert. Because if he can pervert them, then we will make a judgment saying these things were not from the Father."

"When I went to college I was a professional at teaching others how to avoid the Holy Spirit," Ben confessed. "I was very anti-anything that was mystical or different than my tradition. One of the traps I got into was that if I couldn't win an argument that the Holy Spirit wasn't really for today, I'd simply say, 'The Holy Spirit just wouldn't act that way.' That was always my last line of defense. It was a smug little statement that sounded better if you were holding a pipe and looking down your nose: 'The Holy Spirit is a gentleman.' I was clinging to the idea that the Holy Spirit wouldn't do anything that a gentleman wouldn't do."

Doug cracked a smile, "I wish that were true."

"It is the dumbest thing. Now I look back on it and think 'I was in a mental hole.' It worked like this: When someone said they received the Holy Spirit and they spoke in tongues, I would say, 'The Holy Spirit would not make you speak in tongues because He is gentleman.' When people that received the Holy Spirit started playing guitars and singing Vineyard worship songs I would say, 'No, the Holy Spirit wouldn't lead you to do these crazy things.' They would say that when they received the Holy Spirit they fell over. I would say, 'No, no, no, the Holy Spirit would not knock someone over.'

"I had taken the position that I could decide what a gentleman would and would not do. Don't ask me where I got my gentleman's action list, or if I have ever used it in any other life situation. The Holy Spirit, to me, was pretty much a castrated little guy weighing in at about sixty pounds and He just sort of softly moved around a room. He didn't ask anyone to do anything, and He didn't do anything Himself. He was totally useless, but at least I had a smug phrase to totally justify my erroneous view." Ben shook his head at himself, smiling.

Tim hummed, cocked his head, and said, "That's interesting that the intellect was your resistance to the Holy Spirit, and that what you most resisted was the Spirit's power and freedom to move and act and do as He pleased—that's why you needed the 'gentleman' label. You needed it because you didn't trust the Holy Spirit's character. We know the Holy Spirit is as good and as much God as the Father and the Son, but we try to put limitations on what God can do when we fear being out of control, or when we are trying to keep our way of interacting with God on the intellectual plane alone. The Holy Spirit is the part of God that is least easy to confine to a system of beliefs. He's just personal and present and unpredictable. But again we need to trust God's character and God's word about the Holy Spirit, not what men and the enemy and religion have fed us about Him."

"For those of you reading, Ben has realized his mistake and has received the Holy Spirit and does speak in tongues and it has just messed up his whole world in an awesome way," Doug announced.

Doug went on, visibly happy to share about the way he relates to the Spirit, "I like what Ephesians tells us: 'Having believed, you were marked in Him with a seal, the promised Holy Spirit, who is a deposit guaranteeing our inheritance.' One of the things that I like to do when the devil comes to me and tells me that God does not love me is to start speaking in tongues, because when I speak in tongues, it tells the devil that I have an inheritance that he does not have.

"In John it talks about how the Holy Spirit convicts the world of sin and guides me into all truth. He discloses to me what is to come. He glorifies Jesus. He gives to me what Jesus has for me. The Holy Spirit helps me in my weakness. He makes intercessions for me. The Holy Spirit calls people into service and into accountability according to the purpose of what God has. The Holy Spirit teaches us and brings to remembrance those things that Jesus has already spoken to us. The Holy Spirit builds us up. The Holy Spirit encourages us. Sometimes when we don't know how to pray, we don't know how to intercede, and we don't know what to do, we can pray in the Spirit and He will make intercession through prayer.

"I remember in 1974, I was in my tractor plowing and the Holy Spirit filled me. I was praying in the Spirit and making intercession and I just knew I was pulling down strongholds; I was doing warfare in the heavenlies and things were happening.

So I said, 'Lord, this is feeling good. What am I praying? Give me an interpretation of what I am praying.'

"What came out of my mouth when I began to interpret was that I was a prideful, arrogant, self-centered, hardhearted man and I was asking the Lord to deal with my arrogance, to break me, mold me and deal with me.

"Believe me, I don't need any more interpretation after that!"

The whole RV filled with some laughter and short comments about what each might actually be asking for when they prayed in tongues.

"I probably would not have prayed those things and asked for the Lord to do that, but the Holy Spirit was making intercession on my behalf to bring me into the fullness of what God had for me. There have been several occasions where I have prayed for somebody to be healed and the Lord healed them. Then a day or two later that person would come to remembrance and I would feel like I needed to pray. Well, my natural mind would think I needed to pray because something happened regarding the thing about which I had interacted with them, but in reality they were in the midst of a car wreck or they were in the midst of something else and I was praying that God would spare their life in the situation.

"One thing I appreciate about the Holy Spirit, and especially regarding speaking in tongues, is that He prays the perfect heart of the Father in the situation that I am in. That is why the devil doesn't want us to pray in the Spirit. He knows the result of our coming into our inheritance and our coming into the promises of what the Father has for us. What does that do to the devil? It takes back ground that we have given him."

"I was noticing," said Ben, "that you seem to tie receiving the baptism of the Holy Spirit—without any jitter or bump—right into speaking in tongues even though you said that as a teacher, you don't require it. You don't really separate those two things do you?"

"I want all that the Father has for me, so no, I don't really separate them,' Doug answered. "When I received the baptism of the Holy Spirit I asked for the evidence of speaking in tongues because I saw it in the word...and I began speaking in tongues. It's not a requirement for me—I'm going to fellowship with you in Christ, not in experience—but, as we see in Acts 2, Acts 10, and Acts 19, everyone that was filled with the Holy Spirit spoke in tongues.

"I have prayed for people and they have automatically begun speaking in tongues out of a natural flow. It seems to me that the people who have more difficulty with praying in the Spirit are intellectuals who are trying to figure out what is happening to them. But some people just have a childlike faith. They just receive it and say, 'That is my Daddy's gift and He wants me to have it, and I receive it without any complications.' They don't ask if they really need it or how it's going to benefit them. They just enter into it with a childlike faith and receive."

Ben asked another question: "When you are filled with the Holy Spirit can you also prophesy immediately? Can you also teach immediately? Can you give immediately? Can you get words of knowledge immediately? Is there any Scripture that says you cannot get everything immediately?"

Doug explained, "Yes, you can, but you have to accept the things of the Spirit of God. I Corinthians 2:14 says 'The man without the Spirit does not accept the things that come from the Spirit of God, for they are foolishness to him, and he cannot understand them, because they are spiritually discerned.'

"Now, you are asking about the gifts of the Spirit in I Corinthians 12, which are distributed to each one as the Spirit wills. They are word of wisdom, word of knowledge, faith, gifts of healing, working of miracles, prophecy, distinguishing of spirits, various tongues, and interpretation of tongues. There is a distinction between the gifts of the Holy Spirit that we can minister to others with publicly and our personal prayer language. Our personal prayer language enables us to pray and build ourselves up in the most holy faith and intercede and not worry about interpreting it for others, as we see the believers doing together on the day of Pentecost in Acts. That is different than when you are in a congregation and you give a message of tongues. In that case, you have to have an interpretation, as Paul instructs the Church in Corinth to have. One is for personal prayer and the other is for proclamation of what God is doing in a local place."

"I pray in tongues privately much more than I do publicly," said Ben. "I pray in tongues if I am around friends who are comfortable with it themselves. I understand by application the Scriptures say to pray, build yourself up and be encouraged.

"I do believe people get hung up on this one little intersection: 'Why is speaking in tongues so closely related to receiving the baptism in the Holy Spirit?' I think that's a legitimate question, but why make it a *pass/fail* kind of question? It is clear in the Scripture that there is no exact formula but that tongues are just normal for the spiritual person."

Ben looked around, stretched a bit, then smiled.

"Now, I'll throw something out to you, Doug, just for fun. Lately, I have been thinking that it's great if you speak in tongues, but what I really look for as a sign of the baptism in the Holy

Spirit is this: 'Do you cry out to Abba, Father—Daddy God? Do you have the heart of a son?'

"When we see Jesus receive the Holy Spirit during His baptism there was the proclamation of sonship. When Jesus promises the Holy Spirit we read that He will not leave us as orphans. Then it says in Romans and Galatians that when we receive the Holy Spirit that He is the Spirit that cries out 'Abba, Father.' My feeling is that if we just really have to settle on one evidence of the Holy Spirit, as some like to argue for, I would settle on the evidence of the Spirit of Adoption—that calling out to God as 'Daddy, God' is the truest sign of whether or not you have been baptized in the Holy Spirit. How do you feel about that?"

"That is an interesting thought," said Doug. "I think you're right that there will be outward signs of what's going on in our spirits. That's one reason why speaking in tongues is so important because I can show the devil, 'I have received the Holy Spirit.' How do you know you received the Holy Spirit? You asked for it. How do you know you received salvation? Because you asked for it. But then you show outward signs in both instances. I don't think, however, that outward signs can be boiled down to formulas.

"What is the sign of salvation, knowing that you have accepted Jesus? Your old nature is buried in death and you have risen in Christ so that your whole character and nature, the deeds of the flesh, have died. And when the devil comes and questions me about whether I've been baptized in the Holy Spirit, I just begin speaking in tongues and that is a sure evidence of my being baptized in the Holy Spirit and the devil has no more case for argument."

"I like that," said Ben. "We look for signs or expressions that prove what we say that we have walked in and believed in. And if we believe something that we say has power, it ought to have revealed itself in our journey. I'm thinking, though, that what I said about the revelation of the Spirit of adoption being the evidence of the baptism of the Holy Spirit needs to relax a little. This is a lesson for me that every time I try to make a formula out of the expression of the Holy Spirit, I am going to get all tied up in it. I need to quit trying to bring a perfect category to everything."

Doug laughed, "I was ministering in a meeting in a certain denomination many years ago and a young girl had gotten saved. God had saved her and transformed her and I said, 'Now you need the Holy Spirit.' She said, 'Yeah.' So she prayed and received the Holy Spirit and began speaking in tongues and the pastor looked at me and said, 'You sure have made another mess now.'

"So I said, 'What have I done? The girl got saved. She got baptized in the Holy Spirit and she is speaking in tongues. What mess have I made?'

"'Well, she hasn't been water baptized yet.'

"And I said, 'Well, you better get her dunked because she is definitely speaking in tongues.'

"See, their tradition told them you had to be saved and baptized in water before you could receive the Holy Spirit. Well, she had not been baptized in water and here she was speaking in tongues. It messed his tradition up."

"I don't want to get into that formula stuff," said Ben. "I know that God loves me and I know He gives me gifts and I know that the Holy Spirit is a good gift. So I just say, 'Yes.'"

Doug cleared his throat.

"We have looked at the benefit. But what is the work of the Holy Spirit?

"Let's look at people who have received the Holy Spirit. In Acts it says that when they were filled with the Holy Spirit, they began speaking in other tongues as the Spirit gave them utterance. Peter said, 'Repent and be baptized, every one of you, in the name of Jesus Christ for the forgiveness of your sins. And you will receive the gift of the Holy Spirit.'"

"The timing is interesting," said Ben. "One Scripture that really blew my mind was in John 20. It is before Jesus went to the cross, before He was resurrected, before He appeared and taught, and before the disciples went to Jerusalem. It says, 'He breathed on the disciples and said, 'Receive the Holy Spirit.'' I saw that and I thought, 'Oh man. Now, it's all messed up.' I thought I had my timing formula down and now way back then He says, 'Receive the Holy Spirit.'"

"It says they received Him while Jesus was walking with them, and yet they still had to wait for the Holy Spirit at Jerusalem later on. That's deliciously nonlinear," smiled Tim.

"Yes," Ben continued, "I thought, 'Well, if the disciples had to do that, I'm not going to get too freaked out even if intellectually I can't figure all the timing out.' I am just going to say, 'Okay, I have received Jesus but then I am going to ask for the power of the Holy Spirit. I am going to ask for the emersion in the fire that John the Baptist promised that Jesus was bringing. I want it.'"

Tim reinforced what Ben said, "That Scripture helps me understand that you actually can't receive the Holy Spirit statically —only at one time. Some people who have trouble with this say, 'Hey, those guys talking about the baptism of the Holy Spirit are not acknowledging the Spirit that is already in me.' But, I can receive Him in one moment and receive Him more fully in the next moment and that is all okay. I received the Holy Spirit, I receive the Holy Spirit, and I will receive the Holy Spirit. It's similar to knowing that Jesus is always with us according to His promise, but then experiencing His manifest presence is something different entirely."

"I have seen people that have accepted Jesus Christ as their Lord and Savior and as they are being baptized and they come up out of the baptism tank, they come up speaking in tongues," Doug noted, "although nobody said anything about receiving the Holy Spirit. In Acts, Jesus said, 'Do not leave Jerusalem, but wait for the gift my Father promised, which you have heard me speak about.' A lot of people teach that once you get saved, you have all that God has for you. But there are several incidents in Scripture where it is clear that there is a difference between being saved and being baptized in the Spirit.

"One of those passages is in Acts 19, when Paul asks some disciples, 'Have you received the Holy Spirit since you believed?' They replied that they didn't even know there was a Holy Spirit. If you got the Holy Spirit when you believed, it would have been a ridiculous question.

"I think what Jesus did, He did according to what would fulfill the Scriptures," stated Doug. "See, the gift of the Holy Spirit could not be sent until Jesus ascended and was sitting at the right hand of the Father. And I believe that Jesus prepared the disciples when He said to receive the Holy Spirit and also to wait for the power of the Holy Spirit."

"This seems to reflect the truth that you were talking about earlier," observed Tim, "that there is fullness and completeness in Christ's finish work, and yet we still have to appropriate that blessing throughout our lives.

"It says in Philippians," Tim continued, "that we work out our salvation with fear and trembling. That doesn't mean we work for our salvation after we're saved. Salvation has already been attained, but we appropriate it. We work it out. I see this whole Holy Spirit thing in the same way. In a sense, we are receiving the Spirit when we receive the Father's love through Christ's work on the cross because the Spirit proceeds from the Father and the Son. However, we can also appropriate a fuller presence of the Holy Spirit in our lives by saying, 'Yes, I want to receive the baptism of the Holy Spirit.' I might manifest some outward signs of that like speaking in tongues. Even in the days that followed that, I might ask for a greater measure of the Holy Spirit in different areas of my life as I work out my salvation and walk in faith and in fellowship with the Holy Spirit."

Ben looked Tim in the eyes and said, "I have received that even now as a correction. When I was looking at John 20, it did something in me and I said, 'Okay, I have got to deal with what the disciples dealt with. It is okay to wait and receive. It is okay to ask and want more.' That is all I needed when I was in my early 20's to overcome my mental trap that pitted me against the baptism. But hearing what you just said, I need to say: 'I am ready to appropriate and to believe for more of what the Holy Spirit wants to do in my life.' I can't remain in the mentality that I got the entire candy bar when I was twelve years old when I first gave my life to Jesus, or even when I first received the baptism of the Holy Spirit. That is sort of crazy. It is like saying that there is no more to discover of God."

"I think that is a good insight," Doug said. "I also think that God deals with us on the level of where we are at.

"I believe that when I asked Jesus to forgive my sins and save me, I was saved. But in the natural that is the dumbest thing I have ever heard in my life. Someone told tell me that all I have to do is say, 'Jesus, I see that I am a sinner. Will you forgive me of my sin and come in and save me?' And now you're telling me that I am saved and my sins are forgiven? Yet people don't have a problem receiving salvation by praying, confessing their sins, asking Him to forgive them, and believing that God is faithful and just and will forgive. They receive that simply, but some have trouble when you tell them that receiving the Holy Spirit is just the same: You receive the Holy Spirit by asking the Father to come in and baptize you in the Holy Spirit and that once you ask you will receive.' That's that. They say, 'Wait a minute. There has to be more to it than that.' Why? Why do we need to make it more complicated? There wasn't any more to salvation.

Doug looked at Ben and asked, "How did you get saved?"

"I got saved by just praying the sinner's prayer," he said.

"Well, how do you get baptized in the Holy Spirit?"

"I ask the Father for the baptism of the Holy Spirit."

"Well, okay then," said Doug a little loudly, "I'm a selfish person I will confess. I want all that the Father has for me. So if Father has something for me but I don't have it, I'm going to ask Him for it. When I found out that God had the Holy Spirit as a promise for me, I knew I wanted Him.

"Then, when I found out I could speak in tongues, I wanted that, too. I want all that God has for me because all that God has for me is going to help me fulfill His purpose."

"I love the fluidity with which you approach this," Ben said to Doug. "I've watched you over many years have no trepidation around encouraging everyone to receive the baptism of the Holy Spirit, and sometimes I have thought that you had no tact as it related to immediately introducing the baptism of the Holy Spirit to people. I would think, 'Dude, can you wait five seconds?'

However, you never had that reserve. Funny thing is, the results of your immediacy never equated to *bad.*

"Come to think of it," he went on, "I have never seen anybody as result of a simple, direct, non-apologetic, non-complicated, introduction to the baptism of the Holy Spirit fall off of a cliff. In my journey with you, Doug, over all these years I have never seen it equate to bad, weird, dysfunctional or to a rejection of the truth.

Ben continued, "So it has now been proven to me that acting as though the Holy Spirit is no big deal is a mistake. For many years I tried to err on the side of being overly courteous or super slow-paced but it never really helped. So I have really settled into convincing myself and others: 'Why not announce the importance of the Holy Spirit right up front? God loves us!' This is an approach which is way more fun and it doesn't have all of the intellectual pitfalls and complexities that people get their minds all screwed up in."

In a more official tone, Ben asked, "One of the things that I have heard you quote several times from the Scriptures, Doug, and that seems to me to be a bit of a theme is that if one were going to receive the Holy Spirit, that somebody was going to have to lay hands on them. Is that true?"

"There have been a lot of times where somebody laid hands on people and they could speak in tongues, but that doesn't necessarily always have to be the case," Doug answered. "I have known people who had no one to lay hands on them, so they just asked the Father for the gift of the Holy Spirit and they were baptized in the Holy Spirit because the Father is the giver of the Holy Spirit."

"But we don't want to make that a formula either," Ben added.

"No, it seems good, and it is biblical, but it is not a formula. When Ben and I were in Cuba this last year, people were getting the Holy Spirit and speaking in tongues, and the pastor of this particular denomination said, 'It seems like you really have a gift for getting people baptized in the Holy Spirit and speaking in tongues.'

"I said, 'I guess.'

"He said, 'We have not been able to get people baptized in the Holy Spirit and speaking in tongues.'

"Well, we had already discovered their problem," Doug said. "Some men had misrepresented God's gift of the apostolic and so they had formed a hard prejudice against it. Well, the Scripture says that when apostles came in and laid hands on people they were baptized in the Holy Spirit and started speaking in tongues. But the pastor in Cuba had made judgments against the gift of the apostle and had refused to receive them. But when he received Ben and I in our giftings, then the people received the Holy Spirit because the judgments had been broken off. He had allowed judgments to rob his congregation of what God had for them.

"The apostles and prophets are part of the government that God has established for us, as we read in Ephesians. If we don't receive all that the Father has given us, all that Jesus has given us, then we limit ourselves from receiving His gifts. Religion and tradition do that to us. And who is the father of religion and tradition? It is not God. The traditions of man make the word of God of none effect. Not all traditions are bad, but traditions that limit the word of God in you are contrary to the heart of the Father."

"So how do you become baptized in the Holy Spirit?" asked Tim.

"There are basically four things you have to do," said Doug.

"First, you have to believe in Jesus Christ as your Lord and Savior.

"Second, once you become a believer in Jesus Christ you just have to ask him for the baptism of the Holy Spirit that the Father has promised in Jesus' name.

"Third, you just have to yield to that which the Father has for you. Romans 6:13 says, 'offer the parts of your body to him as instruments of righteousness.'

"Fourth, you just believe and expect to receive it by faith."

"That doesn't sound hard," said Ben.

"One reason why people have a hard time speaking in tongues is that they are trying to speak English and most people I know only have one tongue," observed Doug with a half smile. "I can't speak in English and speak in the Spirit at the same time, so I have to disengage my intellect and my mind and allow the Spirit that is within me to have access to my tongue. That confuses and makes problems because my intellect can't figure out what my spirit is speaking. It is not supposed to. My intellect is not speaking. The Spirit is speaking in me. So I have to yield the members of my body to my spirit to allow the Spirit to use that which He wants to."

Tim spoke up, "Regarding receiving the Holy Spirit, I think that, if not a necessary step, probably a great step is—in the same way you receive Jesus and you confess with your mouth and someone witnesses it with you—to either have someone lay hands on you or to confess with your mouth that you have received the baptism of the Holy Spirit as a sign that you have received. I think it keeps us out of that area that we talked about before of wondering what really happened. Then you have a witness that can stir the gifts of the Holy Spirit in you, and when the devil comes and says 'you don't have the Holy Spirit,' you can ask your witness. He or she can remind you.

"Now Doug," said Tim, shifting gears, "to reinforce your belief that the Holy Spirit is an essential foundation for life in Christ, I want to look for a moment to that Scripture in I Corinthians 2 that you read earlier. It says the Holy Spirit reveals to us the depths of God, and that the heart of God can't really be known by the carnal man because it's spiritually discerned. A lot of us who are made new in Christ still walk around with the mind of a natural man, because we've not awakened to our true nature by the Spirit of God.

"But I've loved the Holy Spirit for this lately: The Holy Spirit makes it so that in my redeemed life with Christ, I am new in Christ and walking around doing great things. I don't need to consult any rule book to tell me what to do or have others tell me what the Lord is thinking. The Holy Spirit lets me know the mind of God. I don't need a teacher in that sense of someone to say 'yes' or 'no' or 'that's right' and 'that's wrong.' I have really tapped into something where the Spirit is truly leading me and I feel like I know God's heart as I go about my redeemed life."

Ben laughed and put a fist in the air. "That is way more fun than having to find some mystical code book like the Da Vinci code to figure out what the will of God is. The Holy Spirit has come to take out all that code-ring silliness so that we can just say, 'Hey, look here, the Father is guiding me and leading me. I am seeing the Scriptures like never before and there is nothing else to compare it to.' I don't know how else to encourage the people reading this book other than to say, 'Look, just trust the Father. He loves you.'"

Doug agreed and said, "Isn't that what happened to Paul? It says that after he received the Holy Spirit when it pleased the

Father to reveal Christ to him, he didn't immediately go back to Jerusalem. He didn't immediately go back to the religious world that he knew. But he was led by the Spirit and he was taught by the Spirit. He didn't go back to a place and try to argue it out in his tradition. He allowed the Holy Spirit to bring revelation. We can't filter it through the mindset of our tradition. It is like the air-conditioning unit in my house. If I don't change my filter in my air conditioning unit then what happens? The dirt comes in my house. I think every now and then we just need to change our filter. We need to stop filtering through our traditions, and start filtering through the revelation of the Spirit.

"You can shove any good gift of God into a religious tradition and make it conform. That is what has happened and a lot of people have a bad taste in their mouth because the Holy Spirit has been preached to them as law and formula, instead of as a free gift from the Father.

"I would encourage you if you know Jesus Christ as your Lord and Savior and you haven't experienced the baptism of the Holy Spirit or you haven't even heard of the Holy Spirit just to simply ask the Father for Him in Jesus' name and see what happens. Grace on your journey to receive all the Father has for you in Christ Jesus and the Holy Spirit."

5

BEING IN CHRIST

"If we want it to be warm next time we go camping in the summer, we should go to Oklahoma," said Doug, trying to pick a fight.

"This is warm, Doug," Tim replied in the matter-of-fact way that is used almost exclusively by Colorado natives about this subject.

"Yeah, Doug," Ben agreed as he wrapped a nylon rope around a tree and pulled it tight. A wind gust filled his hammock like wind fills a sail. "All your blood is rushing to your stomach to digest your garlic burger. It's not unlike hypothermia. You'll feel normal again after a nap."

"I've never seen anyone push whole garlic cloves into burgers with a pocketknife like that," remembered Doug, "so I guess you high country boys know some things I don't. It wouldn't be safe to ignore your advice up here in the wilderness, so I'll just submit." He trailed off as he climbed the metal steps, opened the door carefully to keep the wind from blowing it off, and closed it behind him, disappearing into the RV.

Turning his attention to Ben's project, Tim said, "Now that's an interesting hammock. "It's like a black nylon cocoon. Never seen one like that before."

Ben brushed imaginary dust off his hands by clapping them together, a signal that his battening down of the hatches was complete. "This, my friend, is a Hennessy Hammock—with rain fly! They're really light and packable. A lot of guys use them in," he paused, "warmer regions."

"Pretty cool," said Tim, who with some difficulty found the velcro portions and climbed in for a trial run. "Looks like it would keep the bugs off. I mean, if the sixty-mile wind gusts weren't doing it." He climbed back out and grabbed his fleece to use as a pillow on the RV's couch for a nap of his own.

When Tim woke up and stuck his head out the door, it was calm. The ground was wet and the spruce needles were dripping with pure, crystalline droplets sparkling in the afternoon sun. Doug, already awake, bugled like an elk through a paper towel roll as if to announce Tim's arrival. Commanded by the sound, the cocoon suspended between the two trees shifted, shook, and then spilled Ben, wobbly, out onto the ground. He did not look rested, and he seemed a little damp on one side. When asked about his bed-head and the bags under his eyes, Ben admitted that napping in the hammock was a little rough. "I spent the whole time in a place where it's too cold to really rest, but I was too sleepy to have the sense to get up and get another layer of clothing."

Ben seemed to see the comedy in his present state and laughed out loud at himself. "So I pretty much just laid out there and suffered while the wind blew rain into the side of my hammock."

"Well," ventured Doug, "how about we sit you down in the RV to eat some pie and have a hot drink, and then we'll get going on the next chapter?"

Some kind soul had purchased a boxed pie labeled with "Apple," "Caramel," and "Ginormous" at the local supermarket, and had sent it along with the men for just such an occasion. This pie was the reason Ben was looking alive again as he turned on the audio recording device for the next chapter's discussion.

"This chapter is about the difference between believing in Christ and being in Christ," said Doug. "John 3:16 says, 'For God so loved the world that He gave His only begotten Son, that whoever believes in Him should not perish but have everlasting life.' You cannot be in Christ until you have accepted Christ as your Savior by believing in Him. Believing in Christ is the doorway to salvation and it is the access to the Father. Once we have believed, then we need to come into a new understanding of our position of being in Christ. Believing is great, but there comes a time when you have to start being and doing what you believe," Doug said, pausing to emphasize the point.

"In Ephesians 2:10 it says, 'For we are God's workmanship, created in Christ Jesus to do good works, which God prepared in advance for us to do.' So it is not just believing in Christ that we will do these works; it says we are created in Christ and that the works are our destiny—prepared in advance for us to do. Once we have believed in Christ, then we are transformed into Christ. Now we do not just believe about Christ, we believe in and through Christ and we do what Christ has already accomplished.

"Colossians 3 says, 'Your life is hidden with Christ in God.' What God are we talking about here? We're talking of the creator

God, the one that holds the universe in the palm of His hand. Our minds can't even comprehend how awesome and how big God is, but we are hidden with Christ in Him. If we understand this, then how can the devil get to us? The devil has to go through the Father and Christ to even find us. When we have this as our foundation, when we understand our position in Christ, we have passed the point of just believing in Christ.

"In Acts it says it is 'in Him we live and we move and we have our being.' It is not in 'believing about Him' that we live and move and have our being. There is a difference between believing and being."

Doug stopped to make sure Ben and Tim were with him.

Ben, looking as if he were staring at pictures in his mind said, "This has something to do with the location of our identity doesn't it? If I'm in Christ then I've moved from believing about Him to actually being in Him."

"That is—in the robe," added Tim. "I am in the robe of Christ. I don't just believe something about Christ, but I put Him on."

Doug nodded, "Say we are in an RV having coffee."

"And we are," interrupted Tim.

"When people drive through the campsite on the road there, what do they see? Do they see us or do they see the RV?"

"They see the RV."

"That's how it should be when we are in Christ. People no longer see us; they should see Christ. As 'Christ was the radiance of [God's] glory and the exact representation of His nature,' it says in Hebrews 1, we should also reflect the radiance of Christ."

Doug paused and Tim and Ben pondered, as if not expecting Doug to say that.

He continued, "Our identity is not in the things that we do, good or bad. Our identity is in Christ. That is why it's so important to understand the love of the Father and to understand the role that He has called us to walk in—because we are the expression of Christ on the earth. When people see us, they should see Christ. That which radiates from us should be Christ because that is who we are now.

"In II Corinthians 5:21 it says, 'If anyone is in Christ, he is a new creation.' Where are we? We are in Christ. So being in Christ, we become a new creation.

"What else are we in Christ? First of all, we are the righteousness of God in Christ Jesus. God made Him who knew no sin to be sin on my behalf so that I might become the righteousness of God in Him.

"Secondly, we have been made complete in Christ. In Colossians 3:10 it says, 'And in Him you have been made complete. He is the head over all rule and authority.' So I am complete in Christ. I am complete because of what the Father has accomplished in Christ.

"Thirdly, I'm a holy and blameless son of God. Ephesians 1:4 says, 'He chose us in Him before the creation of the world to be holy and blameless in His sight. In love He predestined us to be adopted as His sons through Jesus Christ.'

"We have to get our minds around these things. This is who we are. If I am now in Christ, then I am the righteousness of God —complete, holy and blameless.

"In Romans 8 it says that I am called, justified, and glorified: 'For we know that God causes all things to work together for good for those who love God and those who are called according to His purpose. For those He foreknew, He also predestined to be conformed to the image of His son so that He would be the firstborn among many brethren and those whom He predestined He would also call. And those whom He called He would also justify and those who He justified, He would also glorify.'"

"Those are some staggering truths," remarked Tim. "I'd say a lot of the believers that I know have wrangled out of those promises and have disqualified themselves from that kind of position pretty consistently. But this is our position when we are in Christ. We need to submit to Him and teach our thoughts how to obey!"

Doug agreed and added, "Now you're talking about renewing our minds and coming along to think like Christ as we read in Philippians, 'let this mind be in you that was also in Christ.' If we understand this and understand that we are in Christ, then how can the devil bring accusation against God's love for us and our identity in Him?"

"And now it is time to look at each other with those same eyes. We need to look at each other understanding that we are in Christ," noted Ben.

"Paul goes on in II Corinthians 5 and says, 'Therefore, from now on, we regard no one according to the flesh. Even though we have known Christ according to the flesh, yet now we know Him thus no longer.' He goes on to say that we are not to know one another according to the flesh anymore but to know one another according to the spirit. So when I see you, I should not regard your flesh; I should know you after the spirit—who you are in Christ.

"So if I seek to know a person *according to the flesh*," Ben concluded, "it means that I am not seeing him or her enclosed in Christ's righteousness, and so I will judge them. When we see with our fleshly eyes we are setting each other up for a life of comparison."

"I think seeing each other according to the spirit is looking through the eyes of the Father," said Doug. "It is just like in the natural. I have two children and, Ben, you have two children. Tim will shortly have two children. Our children have some similarities but they have some uniqueness, too. I don't compare one with the other because each one of them is different. That's the way it is in Christ. We are each unique in our gifting. We are each unique in our makeup. This is why we need each other; when we know the family where God has placed us, then every part is important. Because that which you are and do, I can't do. And that which I am and do, you can't do. As each of us do what we can with the grace that God has given us in the function that He has called us to walk in, then the full manifestation of God shows up."

"You stop looking at the old dead man, the person I used to be before I exchanged my life for Christ's life in me," Tim added his two cents. "You start looking at Christ through me."

"Yes," said Doug, looking at Tim. "It is the dying to myself and to what my old nature was and then taking on the image of Christ. So the man that I was is no longer. And who I am in Christ is now what comes alive. I have become a new creation in Christ Jesus.

"What is that *new creation*? In a nutshell, it is that which the Father has predestined for me before the beginning of time. Now the battle that I have is that my old nature is still trying to attain life. That is why I have to take up my cross daily and crucify myself because my old nature is always trying to stay alive and the new nature is trying to birth life. One is passing away and the other is coming forth. In this transition there will be a battle in our minds, so we learn how to rule our minds with the word of God hidden in our hearts, like you said earlier, Tim."

Tim made some notes in his notebook, then tapped it with his pen. "How do you think the person who doesn't know anything about being in Christ or anything at all about Jesus begins to understand how to be in Christ rather than just believing in Christ?"

Doug answered, "I think that is part of the job of the Holy Spirit—to reveal to us the things Christ has done for us and who we are in Christ. If you haven't been filled with the Holy Spirit, you can't understand being in Christ."

Tim nodded, "So we're talking about two natures here, spirit and flesh, at war inside us. And to be in Christ—or to walk according to the Spirit—requires the Holy Spirit because the things of the Spirit are spiritually discerned. I'm referring back to that passage in I Corinthians from our last discussion, and to Romans 8:1 which says, 'There is therefore now no condemnation to those who are in Christ Jesus, who do not walk according to the flesh, but according to the Spirit.'"

"Being in Christ is a process," Doug explained. "As you believe in Christ and as you walk in faith, your mind is being *transnewed* and you are taking on the new image of who you are in Christ. And as you take on that image of being in Christ, then your life is no longer your own. It is in Him that you live and move and have your being, and it is no longer you but Christ in you working though you. You have become one in Christ."

Ben admirably waited for Doug to finish making his point, but couldn't contain his laughter any longer. "I think you just invented a new word, Doug!"

His voice became official, as if reading from a dictionary: "*Transnewed: being both transformed and renewed.*"

Everyone laughed. Ben, not having missed the truth in what Doug was saying, continued, "The more you trust in Christ and the more intimate you become with Him, the more you understand His work and His heart for you. I see myself being moved into an arena where I've realized my entire atmosphere—the entire surrounding of my journey—has changed. My perspective is being changed. I am in Christ. I'm really *in* Him."

"You are now looking through the eyes of Christ as God sees and loves the world," said Doug. "Then some things become clearer, like the Scripture that says that God is not counting our trespasses against us but that He has given us a ministry of reconciliation that we might reconcile men to the Father.

"The natural man only looks at the downfall or the temporal things that he can see. What God has called us to now that we are in Christ is to call forth people's destiny and to know them according to the true identity of who they are in Christ. A lot of times people don't even understand what their purpose or their destiny is. That question is asked all the time: 'What am I supposed to do?' Part of being fathers in the Lord and men and fathers of faith is calling people into their destiny, and the only way to find that destiny is to encourage them to come into an understanding that their life is in Christ. Because their destiny is in Christ. It is not in what they do. It is not in what they don't do. It is not in performance. It is in Christ alone."

"It is easy for someone to think that their destiny is in what they do," observed Tim. "But how could we stay trapped in a performance mentality when we're clothed in Christ?"

"It is called deception," said Doug with no hesitation. "We believe the lie the devil tells us."

Doug looked out the RV window at the afternoon sun. "When we stand before the Father, He is going to hold us accountable for what He's predestined us to be in Christ. If God has given me grace in Christ to be a farmer and rancher and I farm and ranch all my life and only lead one person to the Lord, and out of my farming and ranching income I help people to go on missions or live out whatever my purpose is in the body, that is what I'm going to be held accountable for. My identity is not in farming and ranching, though; my identity is in Christ. Farming and ranching is just the fruit of my identity in Christ; it's what I have grace in Christ to do."

Doug looked at Ben and Tim with a deep sincerity and said, "However, imagine God has called me to be a farmer and rancher and when I get saved religiosity gets on me and I think, 'If I really want to follow the Lord then I have to be a preacher.' Then I leave my farming and ranching and go to preaching. Well, when I stand before the Lord at the judgment, He is going to say, 'I called you to be a farmer and rancher. So why were you preaching and trying to be pastor of a congregation?'

"We have to understand what our identity is in Christ and what God has predestined us to be and get our minds renewed. There may be some men who never preach a message from the pulpit but who are going to do more work in the kingdom than a public teacher might ever do, because in the vocation God has placed them in, they function in the grace that God has given them and in their identity in Christ, all in the midst of the system of the world. And they establish God's kingdom."

"The more that your identity is in Christ," reflected Tim, "the less likely you are to be sucked in other directions and live a life that you are not really made to be about."

"Please be yourself!" Ben yelled with a little too much drama. The caramel from the pie was now definitely in his bloodstream. "If I could just help people that I love be themselves, they would do exactly what you are saying! The King will measure our contributions and our agreement with the kingdom and what He has called us to do based on whether or not we were being ourselves in Christ, not whether we were doing a great job in the eyes of men. A great job in the eyes of the King is doing whatever He has given us to do. And He created us to be perfectly capable of doing it. Our destiny is inside of us and our destiny will work perfectly with being ourselves in Christ."

"I have heard it said that when I stand before God," Tim said with an air of poetry, "He will not ask me why I was not more like Abraham, Moses, David, Ben Pasley, or Doug Roberts. He will instead ask me, 'Why weren't you more like Tim?'"

Ben scraped the last of the pie off his plate as if to celebrate the beauty of this moment in the conversation.

"You're right," said Doug. "But most people can't be themselves because they don't love themselves and they don't know who they are in Christ. They feel they have to work to obtain a place, but the truth is that Christ has already accomplished the good works that God predestined us to do. When Jesus said 'It is finished,' He was saying 'I have fulfilled all that the Father has required.' Jesus paid the debt in full. Our job is exercising faith and calling out of eternity what Jesus has already accomplished and making it known in this season of time that we live in."

"Being in Christ is our destiny," Ben spoke the words simply and waited a moment before going on. "To say that is a very freeing and different thing than to say my destiny is anything else.

"You meet certain people, especially driven or creative ones, and almost always find them trying to find their destiny in their work. I have tried to coach people with this mindset into resting in Christ, but I am often worn out because they are so accomplishment and work oriented. They are always thinking about obtaining the destiny that God has for them by working their craft, and it seems they are never at rest with just being in Christ.

"I think of it like marriage. The goal of marriage is to be intimately married—to be in a deep life relationship. The goal is intimacy and to love your wife or your husband. The goal is definitely not some project you are working on together. You don't get married just to build a house or grow children. It is not working on your kids that helps you be married. Being married is about being together."

"Paul addresses that in Philippians," said Doug. "Look at how much He wants to be together with Christ: 'That I may gain Christ and be found in Him, not having a righteousness of my own that comes from the law, but that which is through faith in Christ—the righteousness that comes from God and is by faith. I want to know Christ and the power of His resurrection and the fellowship of sharing in His sufferings, becoming like Him in His death, and so, somehow, to attain to the resurrection from the dead.'

"The only way we are going to obtain life is in Christ. That is why when you accept Christ you must die to yourself. Your old man—your flesh—dies and your new man comes to life. What is your new man? The man that is hidden in Christ."

"I love that Romans 8 Scripture, Tim." Doug continued. "It says, 'There is therefore now no condemnation for those who are in Christ Jesus.' It doesn't say that there's no condemnation for those who believe. It is those who are in Christ Jesus who have no condemnation on them.

'What this tells me is that when someone comes and tries to put condemnation on me, or when I'm battling condemnation, the first thing that I need to realize is that at that moment I am back in my old self because in Christ there is no condemnation.

God will convict and confront us but God will never condemn us because there is no condemnation in Christ, and we are in Christ."

"So if someone is battling condemnation and guilt, then they need to appropriate the foundations of God's love and forgiveness and come into their identity in Christ," said Tim, enjoying the clarity of his thought.

Doug smiled and went on, "Ephesians tell us, 'He has blessed us with every spiritual blessing in heavenly places in Christ Jesus.' Everything God has blessed us with we find in Christ Jesus. That is why we live in Christ Jesus: so that we can obtain all that God has predestined for us. The workmanship that we are, He created us to be in Christ Jesus. There are a lot of people trying to do good works in the flesh who never get the victory. They are doing all the right things, but nothing ever changes because they are doing it in the flesh instead of doing it in Christ.

"Again, we need to understand that we're robed in the Father's favor just as the prodigal son was robed when he returned home. Everything the Father has for us to accomplish He has called us to in Christ Jesus. It's when we are clothed in Christ that it's accomplished. None of us can do anything in the flesh that will produce eternal things. The only thing my flesh can produce is death. The Spirit, however, can produce eternal life.

"Paul had an understanding that his identity was not in himself. He knew his identity was in Christ. The things Paul did, he did through Christ. The revelations that he had and the ministry that he had were through Christ. He knew he was nothing without Christ. He didn't have millions of people that he was discipling. He didn't have a big organization to join. He said he was the scum of the earth and the chief sinner.

You hear a lot of self-appointed apostles today telling us what it means to be an apostle, but few of them have an understanding of what Paul told us. Paul knew that in his flesh he was nothing, but in Christ he could do all things. His identity was not in the office or the role that he functioned in. His identity was in Christ, in whom he lived. I think I will go with Paul's understanding of being in Christ and what it means to be an apostle."

Doug went on, "If you don't know your identity in Christ and what He has called you to do, then you have to make a place for yourself in your own power. However, I believe that if God knows the hairs on my head, then He also knows my phone number. If He wants me to do something then He will open those doors. I think a lot of times when people don't understand their identity in Christ, then they walk in '*identistry*,' putting their *identity* in their *ministry*. So they always have to promote their ministry so they will feel like they are someone. But once you understand that your identity is not in your ministry but in Christ, then your ministry is just what happens because of who you are in Christ."

"Great point," said Tim. "Doug, you personally helped me out of that hole by believing that I could handle the truth. You told it to me and it hurt, but I needed to have my identity challenged so I could put it where it belongs. I'm also noting that there's another new one for Webster. *Identistry: when you have your identity wrapped up in your ministry.*"

"Some people who have an orphan mentality feel that they need to build things around themselves to give them a place of identity," Ben said. "If you don't know who your family is and you don't know where you belong, you feel like you have to work, strive, and make things to give yourself a home. You have to build your own things out of what you find on the ground. We want to encourage people and tell them that it is fine just to know who you are in Jesus. It means that you are a son of the Father and that you have a place in His heart and it can never be taken from you. That is awesome."

"That is true, Ben, and it releases you from the expectation that you have to build a ministry," said Doug. "There is no place in Scripture where God says to build a ministry. There is also no place in Scripture where God says to build *His* Church, either. Jesus says, 'I will build my Church.'

"When you don't understand the foundations of who you are in Christ, then you have to build something to be someone. Well, when that's the situation, as long as other people accept what they do, they feel worthwhile. But if people reject what they do, then all of a sudden their whole identity is blown."

"If you are not in Christ then you have to find somewhere to park your identity," said Tim. "We are inherently contingent beings. As humans we are always attaching ourselves to something. It is because we were made to be attached to Christ. We were designed to be in Christ and when we are not, we always attach ourselves to other things like our career, cars, success, or our ministry. Attaching our identity to those things is a form of idolatry in our pride. We attach ourselves to Christ then we get free from all those things. They become our servants instead of our masters."

Ben spoke up with some intensity, "More and more young people are taking up the idea of social justice. That is, fixing a social problem or fixing an injustice of some kind. They join every new cause. I know these *causes* are very important. I get it. I'm not diminishing the importance of each one. However, many young people attach their identities to their causes and find their worth in them.

"Also," Ben added, "plenty of young people are attaching themselves to 'building the Church' or 'making the Church.' That becomes their identity: 'I am a reformer.' They write books about how to reform the old and make it new, and why the old one is stupid and why what they are thinking is new, is cool. They let these things define who they are, which is incredibly shaky ground. None of these identities is as cool as finding our identity in Christ and being totally satisfied in that relationship."

"If you understand this," continued Doug, "then you're not easily deceived and led astray from the truth. When you know your identity in Christ then you know the heart of the Father so you're not going to be tossed by every wind of doctrine or scheme of men or led away from the truth.

"When I pray I don't say, 'Good Morning Father. This is your prophet, this is your worship leader, or this is your teacher.' I don't come before the Father in my gift. I come before the Father in my true identity, which is His son!" Doug's voice was raising in pitch which, for him, always revealed that he was excited about what he was sharing.

"What is cool about that is that it sets you free from the rejection and guilt the enemy brings. If someone receives my gift, then praise the Lord. Hallelujah! If someone rejects my gift, then praise the Lord. Hallelujah! They are not receiving or rejecting me because my identity is not in my gift. My gift is just what I do. My identity is in Christ so if someone thinks that I am the greatest thing since the hot fudge sundae, great. If they think I'm the worst thing, then great. It doesn't affect my identity and my ability to walk in faith."

"If you wonder whether you are walking in Christ then," said Tim, "a good litmus test might be this: if someone rejects you, does it cause you to have an identity crisis? If so, you are discovering that your identity is threatened by external circumstances and you might want to consider returning to Christ alone."

"That is a good test," affirmed Doug. "Do you see now how the enemy could come in and rob us of our purpose and our destiny? Because when he robs us of our identity of who we are in Christ then he has automatically stolen our destiny from us. It is very important to believe in Christ, but once you believe in Christ and He becomes your Savior, then you need to come into a place of allowing your mind to be renewed in understanding your position in Jesus. The devil believes about Jesus. The difference is that he is not in Jesus. Just believing about Him is not the answer; it is coming into a place of being in Him. It is in Him that we are going to obtain the fullness of what the Father has called us to be."

"Now this chapter is starting to smoke!" exclaimed Ben. "Before I was in Christ, if I sinned or did something stupid, then my old man used to feel like I needed to strive to do something to earn my way back to my relationship with Jesus. I just knew I had broken my relationship with God because I sinned. However that is a stupid way to understand our relationship with God in Christ. When I sin now that I'm in Christ, I turn to the Father and I realize that He is looking at me, but He is looking through Jesus, which is the robe of favor He has put on me. So I have to take a different way with the Lord. I can't strive. I just say, 'Well now that wasn't like me at all, was it?' And the Lord says, 'No son, that was really not according to your nature. That was according to the dumb spirit.'

"Then I repent because I was not acting according to my nature. I wasn't being who I really am. I don't see myself as being shot through the window into the field of rejection after I sin. I am in Christ when I sin and I remain in Him. He is sharing His reputation all around me so that when I make a mistake, He does not leave me," Ben said boldly and gladly. He continued. "I remember one time when I was on staff with a great pastor, Des Evans, and he said, 'If you make a mistake, I am going to cover you. I'm going to stand in front of you and take some of the shots for you. If you do really well I'm going to applaud and I will be the first man to really celebrate you.' This changed everything about the way I looked at being a leader in the family of God.

"Similarly, Jesus is sharing His reputation with us and when we make a mistake He is going to take the shot for that accusation. He is going to cover us. We don't have to run off alone and try and win our way back to God. Christ is going to stay with us and put His arms around us. I think being in Christ helps us to be able to deal with it when we fail. It also helps us see that we don't need to defend our own reputation because our reputation now is all in God."

"The Father has given us Jesus and He has also given us the Holy Spirit," said Doug. "So what happens when we fall and do something dumb? The Holy Spirit says, 'Hey Doug, that was a dumb thing you did.'

"I agree," chuckled Tim.

"Then Jesus says, 'That's okay, I have forgiven you.' And when the Father sees me, He sees the righteousness of God in Christ because the Holy Spirit did His job of convicting me of my sin and Jesus did His job of forgiving me of my sin, so then I am back in right standing as though the sin never happened.

"Can you imagine what it would be like if the family, the body of Christ, in the city we live in would simply understand what you just said about Christ covering for us and also applauding us as we do well?"

"It would change everything," said Tim. "There would be no division because we'd be building each other up. We'd cover each other and be glad when the other parts of the body were successful. We'd have to have our identities in Christ, not staking out little places and projects to house our significance."

"'For where envying and strife is, there is confusion and every evil work,'" said Doug, quoting James 3:16. "What happens is that because I don't understand who I am in Christ and I see God using you..." He turned his head and gave an example: "Let's say you write this super great song that is given to the Church and it goes worldwide. Then I question why the Lord didn't give it to me. Jealousy comes in and with jealousy comes every evil work. But if I say, 'Hallelujah! Praise the Lord! God, that was a great song you gave to Tim.' Then I am rejoicing with you and then the trap of the enemy cannot lead me astray. But I have to know who I am in Christ."

"I think part of being a reconciler is being able to see people in Christ," ventured Ben. "In that way, you're not judging people. You wouldn't say about someone else, 'On mercy he is about a 70. On listening he's about a 10. On kindness he is a 90.' When we judge people according to the flesh then we operate according to the flesh. Then we share the judgments according to the flesh. When we speak about others this way it uncovers us. It makes us vulnerable because our own weaknesses are then out in the firing line.

"When we see each other in Christ, we are more likely to see a mistake that someone makes and say 'that just wasn't like him.' And so we don't offer a score because that is irrelevant. That person is in motion to perfection in Christ!" Ben said, raising his hands a little like he was going to address a bigger crowd, then he put them back on the table and his tone hushed a little, as if to make a more personal footnote.

"Though I might want to go to that person and talk to them directly about a shortcoming, I really work hard not to share what I might have seen with someone else. There's no reason to do it. Because by the time I get around to talking to that other person about what they did, the Holy Spirit has probably already convicted them and the Father has talked to them about it and they have decided to change their ways. There is no reason for me to uncover what I saw in them before others because it will impart a spirit of judgment. When you see each other according to the spirit, there is more room for someone to not be perfect and still love them well."

Doug agreed, "The bottom line is when I see you by the spirit and not the flesh, you can sin and I just say, 'That's not Ben. That's not who he is; it is just what he did.' But I have to believe that the Holy Spirit is going to do His job, Jesus is going to do His job, and that you are going to come to your senses and realize that was a dumb thing you did."

"And that is a reasonable expectation in the spirit. Not something you would expect from people in their flesh, though. You have to see who they are in Christ and trust the Lord to do the work. It's in His job description," added Tim.

"There is a Scripture in I John where it says, 'If anyone sees his brother commit a sin that does not lead to death, he should pray and God will give him life,' said Doug. "If I know you by the spirit, then when I see you do something dumb I can say, 'Father, that is not that person. Please don't hold this sin to his account.' That brings grace and reconciliation in their life and allows the Holy Spirit to move.

"What happens sometimes though, is that when I see someone's shortcomings, I want to magnify them so people will look at their shortcomings and not see mine," Doug said with a smile.

"So being in Christ or walking in the Spirit, however you want to say it," said Tim, "is not just an individual way to come into a better understanding of who we are, but also a whole way of being together for us, *the Church*. Together, we are also in Christ instead of looking at the dead men that we were before."

Ben made a happy owl sound.

"This is a foundational truth in God's word that would stop lots of the division in the body and stop separation even in husband and wife relationships," said Doug. "A husband might have a legitimate gripe now and then, but if he knows it's not who his wife really is, and she knows that his issues are not who he really is, and they choose not to let the sun go down on their anger, they have reconciliation. The devil doesn't have a foothold there.

"Things happen because people don't understand the foundation of the Father's intention. We are talking about things that the Father predestined for us before He ever spoke the world into existence."

"The intention was to bring us into Christ," Tim said. "We were never meant to be out there on our own where all the worst wounds are inflicted by the enemy."

Tim continued, "In Christ, I can help you to achieve your destiny, despite the things you sometimes do. I see you for who you really are. You might not even totally understand it yet, but when I treat you like that, I call forth more of who you are in your destiny. This is a beautiful thing in any relationship, but especially in a love relationship, and I've been on the receiving end of it. It's honoring to have your faults overlooked and to be treated as the great person that you're not quite acting like. It makes you come into that fullness because it feels so good. I think that is what it means to really *pastor* someone.

"Someone said, 'To love someone is to hope in them forever.' Seeing people in Christ means that you always have a hopeful expectation that they are getting better. We are talking about things that the Lord has already predestined in a person. So even if I'm not much inspired by the way you're acting today, I can treat you like who you really are because I can see you with my faith. Then maybe I'll get to see you come into your destiny with my eyes, too."

Without missing a beat Doug picked up, "In Ephesians it says, 'Do not let any unwholesome talk come out of your mouths, but only what is helpful for building others up according to their needs that it may benefit those who listen. And do not grieve the Holy Spirit of God, with whom you were sealed for the day of redemption.' When we see one another as God sees us in Christ then we are going to quit condemning one another, badmouthing one another, and judging one another. I might hold you accountable but I'm going to speak encouragement to you and call forth life in you as I do it.

"How many people are verbally abused today? They're just beat down until they think they're nothing. All their life they've been told how sorry they are, how worthless they are, how useless they are, and that they are never going to accomplish or fulfill anything.

"When you verbally abuse someone, you are contradicting the heart of what the Father has for them. You sow a seed in their mind that they will never be able to obtain anything because they are worthless. So our job as believers and brothers and sisters is to call forth destiny, and to agree with the Father's intention for that person. You can say, 'I can see a new man. You are awesome. I can see it in you. You are going to be able to accomplish great and mighty things. Your mind has not even comprehended all of the things that God has in store for you.' Isn't that what the word says?"

Ben, in response to Doug's rhetorical question said, "We encourage each other a lot in the art of soul care, gardening in other people's lives or pastoring them. This is one of the most important tools of action that you can take on behalf of someone. You don't have to be someone's overseer; you can just be their friend. There is a little bit of a risk when you step up and say, 'I really see something beautiful in your future.' You are obligated to continue to believe it. You might need to stay ready to partner with them in that and to be alongside them. It is not just giving someone a prophetic word and then leaving and never seeing them again. If you are walking with somebody and you tell them that you really believe in them, then you are agreeing with God's great hope in their lives and in their journey."

Doug nodded in agreement and said, "It says in Isaiah 46, 'I am God, and there is none like me. I make known the end from the beginning.' Part of what you're talking about is seeing the end of what God has for someone to be in Christ. God might say to someone that He has called them to be one thing but they might only be able to see where they are or what they are doing at that moment. But as Paul said, 'Our light and momentary troubles are achieving for us an eternal glory that far outweighs them all.' We are calling forth out of a temporary mindset the eternal purpose that God has predestined for them, and it is helping them lay hold of the vision that is before them so they won't be distracted in the momentary things. We help them understand that the things they are going through are conforming them to the eternal purpose that God has called them to."

"Don't let present circumstance and environment dictate who you are," advised Ben. "You have to hear what the Father's talking to you about. A few words later in Isaiah the Lord says, 'My purpose will stand and I will do all that I please.' He is the Father and ultimately what He has spoken will stand.

"Amen, that is good," said Doug. "The sad thing is that I can hinder God's purpose in my life by choosing not to believe what He said about the end. When I make a judgment or believe a lie of the enemy instead of the truth of what God has spoken to me, then my life can be robbed of what God has predestined for me because I choose to walk away from what is true. When we agree with the Father by entering into Christ, then no weapon formed against us will prosper. No plans set against us can succeed.

"Ask the Holy Spirit to reveal to you who you are in Christ, and then begin to walk it out by faith in what the Father has spoken concerning you."

6

FOUNDATION NUMBER SIX:

PRACTICING RIGHTEOUSNESS

"San Juan Worm," said Ben, probing a short, red, fuzzy string attached to a hook in Tim's fly box. They rocked gently back and forth in the canoe, having paddled close to the mouth of the creek that fed the reservoir. Small waves lapped at the canoe's sides.

Tim frowned at Ben's fly selection. "Everyone knows Jesus' closest disciples were dry-fly fisherman, and that is not a dry fly. That's the next thing to plunking a nightcrawler out there with an all-you-can-eat sign taped to his back."

"Okay, quality over quantity then," shrugged Ben. With leftover winds from the afternoon storm still sending the occasional sheet of shimmering white across the lake in the distance, the conditions were not quite as ideal as in the previous evening. Still, the immediate area seemed calm enough.

They selected a few patterns and Tim slipped the box into his vest. As he tied the first fly on, a trout could be heard raising not ten feet from the boat. He tied faster. "How about if we paddle up to that seam between the current and the calm on the other side there?" Tim asked Ben as he tugged his fly to check his knot.

As Ben put the paddle to the water, two more fish jumped in that exact area.

Tim glanced behind him and started casting. Slow and U-shaped, the line went back, then forward. Back, then forward. The fly could be heard resisting the slight breeze. All at once, the bright green line slapped the water, followed by the fly.

Ben and Tim watched the fly drift with the current. It was a long drift, and Ben paddled the boat occasionally to stay near the interesting water.

Nothing.

He pulled his line and cast again, this time right to a hefty rainbow trout who had risen in the steadier current during the backcast.

"Wait for it," Tim coached the fish as the fly touched down and turned downstream. "Ah!" He yelled instinctively as he pulled his line forcefully from its resting place on the water's surface, "missed 'em!" He turned his failed strike into another quick forward cast. Two or three fish now worked the edge of the eddy.

Still a little unsure how to move or shift his weight in the canoe, Tim's next cast rocked the boat a bit, and he watched his line pile up in front of him. He punctuated his dissatisfaction with a "harrumph."

He continued casting and in short order brought two or three smaller trout to hand, even on imperfect casts. "Seems like I'm missing the bigger ones," he said to Ben, who he knew would have some helpful advice or at least could be trusted to invent some on the spot.

"They don't get that big eating just anything that washes down the stream," responded Ben, now letting the boat drift along the shore and away from the reservoir's source. White insects could be seen hovering above the water's surface against the dark background of the shadowy shore.

"Look, Tim. You're a bug. You're not going to dive-bomb the water. It's not how you behave. You're going to settle down on it gently so you can fly away in a while. Here's what my dad says: Aim your cast as if you were trying to get it to land one foot above the water instead of right on the surface."

Seeing the image in his mind, Tim cast again toward the shore. The line extended beautifully, hovered for a split second, then fell lightly on the water—first the fly, then the line. "Marvelous!" Ben said in a hushed tone that was filled with expectation.

They watched the fly drift gently at the same pace as the boat. The surface reflected the first stars, the insects danced, the water sloshed on the bank. Transfixed, Ben and Tim waited.

Tim took a deep breath, remembering the feel of the previous cast. In his mind's eye, he saw the line extend in the same beautiful way; then he did what he felt inside. He brought a trout to hand.

As he continued casting this way, he stopped thinking about the line, the one foot above the water principle, or the fly's gentle settling. It was becoming second nature and felt great.

Suddenly, Ben let out a "Whoop!" Tim felt the line settle in the boat, and looked with embarrassment while Ben removed the fly from the back of his collar. "Don't worry about it," he said as he repositioned the canoe to get out of the way of Tim's back cast. "My fault, really."

Tim sent a near perfect cast out into some quiet water on the lake side of the canoe. This time, a "gloop" could be heard the moment the fly touched the water, followed by the buzzing sound of the drag in the reel. A monster fish was taking the fly out to deep water!

Landing that fish was the perfect ending for a perfect evening fishing trip.

Ben and Tim, finally at the mercy of the evening and with no help from the waning moon, pulled the boat ashore and stashed it in the woods. They recounted landing the big lake trout as they ascended the slope and climbed into the RV.

Doug was ready when they arrived. Without much warm up he clicked the recorder on as Ben and Tim took their shoes off and got comfortable in their chairs.

"A few years ago the Lord was speaking to me about what I am practicing. When I thought about it, I realized that part of the trap of the devil was to trick us into putting our identity in what we might do, instead of who the Father has called us to be in Christ.

"I have noticed that when people sin, the devil comes immediately and puts shame and condemnation on them so they will have an attitude like, 'What's the use? I will never be able to make it. I will never be able to be what God has called me to be because I always keep doing dumb things.'

"As we've been talking about together, the devil always tries to put our identity in what we've done instead of in who we are in Christ. The devil is always there to accuse us when we mess up. He tells us, 'This proves who you really are.' I believe if he can deceive us into believing that our identity is in what we have done, then we will always be battling an identity crisis because we do make mistakes. The devil says, 'Well, you did it again so that is just who you are.' We have to understand that we are going to make mistakes. We are human."

Doug smirked and kept talking, "I was told once, 'if it is worth doing, it is worth making mistakes doing it.' God knows our hearts and He can fix the mistakes. Remember, it was God that first loved us and chose us to do good works on the earth. He chooses imperfect people to accomplish His perfect will. We take up our cross daily, dying to self, and we become more like Christ. The more we behold Him, the more we become like Him. Can you imagine the authority and the power that we would have if we didn't agree so quickly with the lies of the enemy and we'd begin to believe the truth of what the Father says about us?"

Doug looked at Ben and Tim, who appeared inspired, but he wasn't about to stop. "'See how great a love the Father has bestowed on us, that we would be called children of God; and such we are,' he read from I John. 'For this reason the world does not know us, because it did not know Him. Beloved, now we are children of God, and it has not appeared as yet what we will be. We know that when He appears, we will be like Him, because we will see Him just as He is. And everyone who has this hope fixed on Him purifies himself, just as He is pure.'

"I don't believe this is talking about the rapture; it is not when we behold Him in the air. It is as we are beholding Him in our day-to-day walk and in our day-to-day relationship here on the earth, where as I see Him I become more like Him. As He reveals Himself to me, I am conformed into the image of who He is. This is the hope that purifies me," Doug repeated, "I'm being conformed into the image of who He is.

"Then it says, 'Everyone who practices sin also practices lawlessness; and sin is lawlessness. You know that He appeared in order to take away sins; and in Him there is no sin. No one who abides in Him sins; no one who sins has seen Him or knows Him.'

"That just blew me away. I know that I have beheld Him. I know that I know Him. I know that I have been saved. I know what God has done in my life, yet here it says that no one who sins has seen Him or knows Him. I told the Lord that I didn't understand because I have sinned, yet I know that I know Him and I have seen Him.

"Then it goes on to say, 'Little children, make sure no one deceives you; the one who practices righteousness is righteous, just as He is righteous; the one who practices sin is of the devil; for the devil has sinned from the beginning. The Son of God appeared for this purpose, to destroy the works of the devil. No one who is born of God practices sin, because His seed abides in Him; and He cannot sin, because He is born of God.

"That began to bring in a whole new revelation.

"I have made a choice. I practice righteousness."

Ben made a grunting sound of agreement that did not break Doug's stride.

"Every now and then I might do a dumb thing but that dumb thing is not who I am, it is just the thing I did. I am born of God so my heart is to practice righteousness. 99% of the time what I practice is righteousness, but 1% I might mess up and do a dumb thing. In that 1% the devil comes in to deceive me and tell me that the 1% is who I really am. I have to remind myself and tell the devil that I am in Christ and in Christ there is no sin. Like I said, that is just what I did but it's not who I really am."

"There is a difference between who I am and what I have done," Ben affirmed.

"The bottom line is that if we have a heart to know the Father and to fulfill His will then we are all practicing righteousness because that is our heart. Why is that? It is because He is righteous and in II Corinthians 5:21, the word says that we are the righteousness of God in Christ Jesus. If we are in Christ Jesus then our hearts, our mentality and our life is practicing righteousness.

"The devil is not our father.

"There was a season when the devil was our father and we were obligated to sin. But we are not obligated to sin any longer because the devil is not our father. However, the devil is always trying to get us back in the mentality that we are his children instead of children of God. The passage in I John continues: 'By this the children of God and the children of the devil are obvious: anyone who does not practice righteousness is not of God, nor the one who does not love his brother. For this is the message which you have heard from the beginning, that we should love one another.'

"Can I make a couple of observations here?" asked Tim. "First, this passage more than once reminds us that we are the children of God. That's how it addresses us. It's as if the author John knows this is going to be a tough one, and that we're never going to make sense of it if we don't remember that we're Daddy God's kids. This is definitely more than being a generic child of creation; he is speaking of our sonship through Christ. That is the basis of the whole argument. Then, it says that God's seed is in us —that we have His DNA now, and that's why we can't sin. There is no sin in Christ, and that's where we are! This reminds me of how we should be able to see outward signs of our inward spiritual states. When we lean out of Christ we can act like we're not God's children and that's when things get wonky and the wires get crossed. That doesn't change our identity though, as the devil would have us believe. That's when we must remember we're children of God and to practice being who we are—we must *practice* righteousness."

Doug nodded and looked back at his open Bible to repeat from I John 3, "'This is how we can tell them apart. The one who is practicing righteousness is righteous; he is from God. The one who does not practice righteousness is not from God.'

"You can look at people that confess to be believers but whose life is just a continuum of practicing unrighteousness, and you can question whether they've ever had a salvation experience. But you take someone who is practicing righteousness but every now and then messes up—again, that is one of the reasons we don't know one another after the flesh but after the spirit—well, those mess ups are just what he did, not who he is. When we focus on what he did in the flesh instead of who he is in Christ, which is spirit, we will miss the heart of the Father for that person. The heart of the Father is always to restore; the heart of the devil is to destroy."

"If you have come to know Christ, to trust in Him, and you are walking in Him it can still take a while for living a life of unrighteousness to drop off," said Ben. "That doesn't mean you don't know the Lord because it's taking a while for it to drop off and lose power. There are also certain people who have run into seasons or stresses that happen to them in their journey, and they just go nuts for a short time in sin and start acting like a crazy person. Also, there can be certain people who struggle with an addiction and the devil really gets on them about it...even though they're trying to practice righteousness. When you take these three types of people struggling with old sin habits, seasons of craziness, or addictions—do you treat all of those people the same or do you treat them differently?"

"I think we are creatures of habit," Doug responded. "When someone has walked in the world twenty to forty years and all of a sudden comes into a place of knowing the Lord and experiencing God's love, they still have habits that they have formed through those years. Even when they come in to a place of embracing a life of believing in Christ and coming into Christ those habits may continue.

"It is the 'kindness of God' that brings repentance. God's love is what breaks the habits. It was God's love for me and not God's judgments against me that broke me out of my habits. God brought me to a place of knowing His love, and then He could say that what I was doing was not pleasing Him. I would tell the Lord that I didn't know what I was doing was sin, and I would repent. God is not so much concerned with the outwardness of what we do; He is concerned with the inwardness of why we do it. He lets us be confident in His love for us, and then deals with our heart issues.

"When I first got saved, as we talked about before, I had a drug habit and did a lot of things that weren't good. But when I experienced God's love, there were things that I immediately quit because I already knew inside me that they weren't right. And God also took away the desire for them. I went from a $300 a day cocaine habit to not doing cocaine overnight because of my salvation experience, but yet I was still doing other things. In my walk with the Lord, the more I beheld Him the more I wanted to be like Him. In the process He would tell me that certain things were not really like Him. He knew my heart and the new man that wanted to be like Him so He would love me in those areas and I would change. He did not judge me and come in and say, 'Well if you love me then you can't do this and that.' The temporary things that I was doing had nothing to do with the eternal purpose that He had called me to do. Knowing His love for me over a season of time dealt with my habits that I had formed before I knew Him and change came to my life."

"The shift in your identity later began to change your behavior," observed Tim. "We have to realize that we deal with two natures: the old nature that is dead but sort of fighting to surge back up, and the new nature. It would be easy for some people who would focus on behavior to read this Scripture and to use it to be robbed of the validity of their faith. I think that it is speaking to our identity first, and then to the behavior that flows from that. Not the other way around. If we could achieve being born of God by good behavior, the author wouldn't keep reminding us that we're already children by the lavish gift of God's love. I think this is a real life-giving verse when you realize that it is saying that in your new identity and the way that Christ expresses Himself in you, you should expect not to sin."

"And when you sin you immediately look at it and say, 'Lord I am sorry,'" added Ben. "'I shouldn't have done that because that is not who I am.'"

Tim continued Ben's thought, "Then you go back to practicing living from who you are in Christ: *God's beloved son.* We expect children to reflect who their parents are because they are of the same seed or substance, and that's what this Scripture is trying to teach us!"

"Yes, you are getting it," said Doug.

"This will be my thirty-fifth year of walking with the Lord and being filled with the Holy Spirit. Things that used to be a temptation to me are not even an issue to me now. Stuff I battled with when I was in my 20's are not even a thought in my 50's. Part of that is that I grew in the Lord and part of it is the time clock. As a person grows and matures, things that were issues are no longer issues.

"Part of practicing righteousness is renewing your mind. James tells us that when you have a thought—a temptation, let's say—there are one or two things you can do with it. You can either take that thought captive by the word that is in your heart, or you can let that thought become an action. Once the thought becomes an action then the action becomes sin. The thought itself is not a sin, but when the thought becomes an action then the action becomes a sin. If we take every thought captive by the word that is hidden in our heart and filter it through Christ, then we can decide not to let the thought become an action. It says, 'Let this word dwell in you. Have this mind in you.' It is what I let rule me at that particular time that is going to either produce righteousness or produce sin."

Ben lowered his finger onto the table like the needle on a record player lowers onto the record. "When you are dealing with habits it is similar to a phonograph record," he said. "If you let the needle sit on that record long enough it will dig a groove in that thing and won't come out to play the rest of the song. The good thing is when Jesus comes in and starts restoring us, He can fill up those grooves and we don't have to stay in those same habits.

"An example is this. Perhaps you have walked with the Lord and you feel that you have pretty much choked out all the old sin habits, but then something happens. Say you are an artist, for example, who lived your whole life without a struggle with pride because you never did anything that people applauded," Ben smiled. "Then one day you paint a painting that people really start to praise and all of a sudden you realize that you are having a tremendous problem with being prideful. You start to be condescending toward other people's art. I think that new situation reveals your heart and now it is time to repent and choose who you are really going to be: the prideful artist or the one whose reputation is found in Christ alone."

"Ben, I think that is very true because each and every heart is different," said Doug. "What is temptation to you is foolishness to me and what is temptation to me is foolishness to you. That is why we are to encourage one another and strengthen one another instead of judging one another.

"Sometimes I think God doesn't necessarily close His eyes to what we do but that He kind of overlooks it because He knows that it's really not the issue of who we are, it was just a dumb thing we did and the Holy Spirit is going to do His job and convict us. Then Jesus is going to do His job to forgive us. Then next week it's not even going to be an issue because God knows our hearts."

"As a kid I was riding in the truck with my dad once," remembered Tim. "Maybe I was in seventh grade. My dad forgot something and I told him how dumb he was in a joking kind of way. I was just trying to find my way as a young man, and I thought, 'Hey, it would be cool if I could make fun of my dad.' It was totally disrespectful and he probably thought it was just weird and unlike me. Well, he knew he wasn't dumb, and he also knew that my heart wasn't to degrade him, so he just didn't say anything about it. We just went on. And he never did bring it up. Well, the Lord started working on me about it and I was convicted that that's not the way I should talk to my dad, and so I never talked to him with disrespect again. My dad overlooked the offense and the Lord did His job. I guess I never actually apologized for it, because we just knew each other's hearts and it didn't matter. But here you have it in writing now, Dad. Sorry."

"That's a good story," said Doug. "Getting back to Ben's question about addictions and habits—if it's a case where the guy is continually doing something over and over again, he might need to have some deliverance. It might be a demonic thing that he just cannot shake loose and he needs to be delivered. In that case it wouldn't be a habit that he has to get over, it would be a demonic stronghold that he needs someone to come in and help him be delivered from. But we'll talk about demonic strongholds more in a second. First I want to keep talking about Tim's issues," Doug laughed at himself as Tim rolled his eyes.

"If I see that someone, Tim, let's say," Ben said with a smirk, "is having a problem with being arrogant and he is starting to get a critical spirit on him, then I would go to the Father and ask Him about it. I would also ask that person, "What is it in you that is telling you that you don't measure up?' What I'm trying to do is get at the root of what is revealing itself through his critical attitude and the condescension toward others that is coming out of him. There is a way to help one another to overcome sin that is better than just pointing out the sin. You know that if sin comes up in the life of a believer, it is rooted in something that is giving it life."

Doug agreed. "Most people deal with the outward expression but never deal with the root. If you never deal with the root, the expression is going to manifest in different forms. You take a man that is dealing with the spirit of alcoholism, it will manifest in two ways. He will be either a teetotaler or he will be a complete drunk. It is the same root.

"One man might be afraid that if he takes one drink he would swing completely out of control so he becomes a teetotaler, but he is still battling alcoholism. On the other hand, the other guy just gives in to it and becomes a total drunk. It is the same root. It is not how much he drinks or how much he doesn't drink. It is the power that he gives the drink to master him. We are so temporal in our relationships we want to sugarcoat things because we don't want to deal with the real issues. It takes commitment, love, long-suffering, endurance, patience and all those things to help a brother out of a bad situation that he might be in. Sometimes, unfortunately, we think it is just more convenient to point out the sin and we believe that that is our duty.

"I think of the Scripture in Hebrews that talks about submitting to those who watch for your soul. Remember, a man's soul is basically his *mind*, his *will*, and his *emotions*. Sometimes it is the soul that we have to address in the person. When you deal with a soul issue then the expressions of sin may continue to be a problem. The soul is more of what is on the outside as it relates to who we are. You know, we are now spiritual men and that is our core. When we deal with healing the roots, the spiritual core, the plant will begin producing good fruits. God deals with our heart issues, and then our outward expression changes.

"In my situation, I was still doing some things that I shouldn't have been doing after I accepted Christ. But the Holy Spirit was still speaking to me and Jesus was still revealing Himself to me through His word. Then there came a time when God decided to deal with these things that were in me. When He dealt with the root of what was causing me to do the things, I changed. It was because He loves me that He decided to deal with my issues. God has never condemned me for anything that I have done. He has disciplined me, but His disciplining me was because I was His son that He loves.

"Acts 14:22 says through much tribulation we will enter the kingdom of God. God chastens, or disciplines, those He loves. When I see a man without discipline it tells me he is fatherless. We all have children and we discipline our children when they do something that is going to cause them harm. We don't want them to hurt themselves so we bring discipline out of our wisdom that they don't have at a young age. If you understand who you are in Christ, then when you go through the process of discipline and the devil comes to you and says that God doesn't love you or these things wouldn't be happening, then you can say to him that he is wrong. God does love you so much that He disciplines you so that you will be more like Him."

Ben had a look of joy on his face thinking about his boys and said, "As parents we don't just discipline to fix our children. I discipline my children so that they know who their daddy is. I want them to really know who they are. I hold my sons by their little faces and remind them of who they are. I ask, "Whose son are you?" I make them answer the question.

"They say, 'I am your son, Dad.' Sometimes it's after I have had to discipline them and I ask them, "Do you understand that I am your dad?"

"'Yes.'

"'Then why do I discipline you?'

"I make them talk about it. I don't want them to get lost. I don't want them to be the sons of intellect or tradition or principle. I want them to be *my* sons. In the same way, our Father isn't willing to just submit us to the principles of Christianity. He doesn't want us to be raised and tutored by the teaching of what is right and wrong. He wants us to know that He is *our* Father. He wants to deal with us in a way that we don't confuse it."

"That is because we are His expression on the earth," said Doug. "God is not a religious God. He's a relational God and He is spirit. For all of our lives we have been preached at with religion but never have been taught spirituality. Jesus was not a religious man. He was a spiritual man. That is why the religious people could not hear what He was speaking. He was speaking spiritual things to religious men and religious men can't comprehend spiritual things. So many times the world and the enemy try to put religion on us. Then people start to come to a meeting only once a year to be revived, and then a year later they need to be revived again because there hasn't been any foundation laid. Revelation is a great thing. But if you don't have the foundation, how can you walk in the revelation? We have all these promises available from the Father that He has given us but if we never tap into them, what use are they to us? The devil always tries to keep our identity on something different than who we really are."

"When we come into the family of Jesus everything changes," said Ben. "There is something very beautiful about a family that has learned to remind each other who they really are. You need to be reminded of who you really are when you drift off into mental traps. Say you get hit with a crisis and you go off on your own, in your own power, to try and fix it. If your job drops off and your finances dry up and you begin to trust yourself instead of the Father, then you are heading off into this trap. If you don't have someone to remind you who you are, then you are alone and in trouble. Sure, the Father is going to talk to you and remind you that He loves you, but we put ourselves at a disadvantage in dealing with our sin struggles and our brokenness when there is no one close enough to remind us of who we really are. We must give some people permission to do that. I have to give that permission to you, Doug, because you are my pastor."

"If you don't have those relationships then the devil comes in and puts guilt on you about doing the same thing over and over again and tells you that you are not really who you think you are. If you don't have someone confirming who you are, then the devil is quick to confirm who you're not," said Doug.

"You can start feeling defeated and give up on having faith because you don't think there's any victory in it. You let the enemy define you by your behavior in the midst of a near-impossible situation that you presented yourself to," added Tim.

"I need people to help me remember," sighed Ben. "I know a lot people spend Sundays going to a meeting, sitting in a room with a lot of people, but still don't have anyone who is near enough to remind them of who they really are. They have no one to speak hopeful words about them and their growth in Jesus. I wish I could wave a wand in those situations and have people connect to each other instead of connecting to just a meeting."

"In I Corinthians 14, Paul compares the Church to the members of the body," explained Doug. "In our natural body we have to be connected or joined to other parts because life flows through the connections. If I cut my hand off, is it still part of my body? Yes, it is part of my body but it is not functional because there's no life flowing to it. What happens to a part of your body that is cut off? It begins to dry up and stink. So many times we have isolated ourselves from the body that God has connected us to, and when you isolate yourself you really come into the trap of the enemy. He will just bombard you with lies and accusations of guilt because there's no life flow there to speak life into you. When a person disengages from the body or family that God has connected them to, then it is almost like cutting the hand off. You still have a hand but it is useless because there's no life flow there."

"It's hard to practice righteousness when you're dried up and stinky!" repeated Tim. "So again we see that this foundation isn't something you practice in a vacuum; it's a way that we need to relate to each other in the Church."

"We are always in peril of the devil taking advantage of us if we are not together and growing in relationships with each other," said Ben. "Bob Terrell used to share an illustration about being fit together as the body of Christ. He would quote Hebrews 10:25 from the King James: 'Not forsaking the assembling of ourselves together.' Then he would say if you put a bunch of pieces of a toy together in a box, put it under a Christmas tree, and put a sign on the box that says 'some assembly required,' then when the child opens it on Christmas morning there is not much she can do with it. Just because all the pieces are in a box does not mean it is assembled together. A lot of people still preach 'not forsaking the assembling of ourselves' to mean 'don't stop meeting in a building once a week.' That's a pretty poor interpretation for that Scripture. We ought to be fit together in relationships 'joint to joint' like it says in Ephesians 4. We can really supply and encourage each other when we are not just loose pieces in a box but pieces that are actually fit together."

"I think that's right. Are you practicing family or are you practicing religion?" asked Doug. "When you are practicing family, you invite people into your home and into your lives —'Let's have a cup of coffee or have lunch.' If you are practicing religion, you invite people to come to your building and hear your preacher. Are you practicing a life of family connectedness or a Sunday morning experience? Are you inviting people to a building or are you inviting people into your life?

"Don't misunderstand what I am saying here. I am not against meeting in buildings. But we know that buildings are not the Church. People are the bride that Christ is coming for, not a stone building. We need to understand they are two totally different invitations. When you invite people to a building you don't have to have a relationship with them or a commitment to them. You invite people into your family you are inviting them into your life."

"On one hand," said Tim, "when people come into a building to get together and to worship the living God, how can that not be awesome? But," he lowered the volume of his voice, "you can go to a large meeting with 10,000 people or a meeting of 10 people and still be totally alone."

"It is not a guarantee is it?" asked Ben. "I like getting together with friends for prayer and worship. Obviously, that part of the Scripture is plain—we are to come together for meetings. But most people think because they go to a meeting once a week that they have fulfilled the Scripture, but that's pretty far down the list for what the expectations of what a family can really be like."

"If you compare the Church and the world," said Doug, "there are just as many divorces in the Church as there are in the world right now. I'd dare to say that is because they go to the building but they don't go to the family. They go to hear a message. Because they hear it they think they have it but there is no application. What are they practicing? They're practicing what they were before they came and heard the word. When they go out it is stolen from them. They are hearers but not doers. They are believing but they are not being.

"In the last chapter we talked about how once we believe, then we begin to be. When God speaks to us something and we acknowledge that we believe it, then we need to begin doing what we believe He says. Most people miss out because they hear what they believe is the Lord but they never bring the application of what they believe into practice by being it. So the devil comes and robs us. What benefit is it if you don't put into application what you believe the Lord is saying to you? It is like salvation. I believe that it's God's will that all should be saved, but if I never appropriate what I believe by receiving new life through faith, then I will go to hell.

"Now getting back to what I was saying. What is sin? Sin is missing the mark. Some people think sin is if you get into an adulterous affair or rob a bank. Those are sins, they say, with a capital S. They reason to themselves, 'Well, I don't do that,' as though that is a good excuse for what they actually do. People think they can justify their sin because it's really not that bad or it's not hurting anybody. It is still sin, however. What are you practicing? You could be practicing religion and still not know the Father. What are we giving ourselves to? I ask people, 'If they started arresting Christians, is there enough evidence against you that they would know that you are a believer?'"

"That is, if they are using something other than an attendance scale," smiled Ben.

"Can your neighbors tell by your lifestyle that you are a son of God and there is something different about you?" Doug questioned. "Or do you just blend in by only going to a building every Sunday morning?"

"I had a relative," Ben said, "who came to visit us from across the state. We were having this wonderful family time with children and grandchildren but this person had to jump in their car and go to Sunday School on Sunday morning. It was with people she didn't know in a place she'd never been to. Why? She had never missed a morning of Sunday School in her life and it wasn't going to happen that Sunday. It was the idea of being threatened by the loss of the Gold Star of Attendance that kept her serving that tradition. She gave up true family intimate time to go serve that tradition and get that recognition."

"That is sad," said Doug. "That reminds me of Mark 7, where Jesus said, 'These people honor me with their lips, but their hearts are far from me. Their worship of me is empty, because they teach human rules as doctrines' [and] abandon the commandment of God and hold to human tradition.' It saddens me that people are so bound up in the traditions of men that they miss the opportunity to be with family, which is the Church.

"On another note," continued Doug, "in Romans Paul says, 'Even so consider yourselves to be dead to sin, but alive to God in Christ Jesus. Therefore do not let sin reign in your mortal body so that you obey its lusts, and do not go on presenting the members of your body to sin as instruments of unrighteousness; but present yourselves to God as those alive from the dead, and your members as instruments of righteousness to God. For sin shall not be master over you, for you are not under law but under grace.'

"Part of practicing righteousness," he explained, "is what we present ourselves to. I believe that the authority of the kingdom of God is within us, but if I keep presenting myself to an awkward situation or a perverted situation, sooner or later something is going to happen to me. It is important to guard our hearts and to guard our minds in what we present ourselves to. What do you engage in? What do you like? What is your mindset? If I hang out with people who have a passion for the Lord, it is going to get in me. It is what I present myself to that I allow myself to embrace.

"Years ago Rita and I were going to minister in Austin, Texas. I saw a billboard advertising something that was not righteous. As I was driving by I heard this voice saying, 'You need to go there. You will enjoy that.' Now I'm on my way to minister the gospel and the devil is attacking my mind with these thoughts. I have learned that I have to rule and take my thoughts captive. I said, 'No, there is nothing in that place I would enjoy. There is nothing in that place that would fulfill me.' What happens when we don't understand the principle of ruling our thoughts and what we practice and present ourselves to, is that ten years down the road I might have found myself in a place like that wondering how I got there. In that case, the seed or thought that the devil planted would have taken root and then, when the opportunity presented itself and I presented myself to that opportunity, I would start practicing sin."

"A thought-seed left on the ground unattended can still grow if not taken captive," said Ben. "On a very basic level, if you hang out with people that whine and complain all the time, then you are going to become a whiner and a complainer. It is just impossible to get away from it. If you hang out with people who have critical spirits and judgmental spirits then you are going to become critical and judgmental. There is a principle there. We are not to isolate ourselves and hide away from everything, but what we can do is be aware of the people we are hanging out with and the subtle influences that they will certainly have."

Doug nodded, "We have to know that 'greater is He that is within us than he that is in the world,' so we don't conform to the world. We allow the world to conform to us. It really grieves my heart, and I believe it grieves the heart of the Father, that we have tried to make our meetings sinner-friendly instead of just presenting the righteousness and love of God and watching Him change peoples' lives. Some popular methods are contrary to the word of God.

"Some people say that God is a God of love and we just need to love everybody. Yes, but you love everybody into the truth. If you love somebody you are going to tell them the truth. If you love somebody you are going to bring them into the destiny of who God has called them to be. You don't conform or compromise the gospel just to get a bigger crowd."

"It's one thing to have a culturally relevant expression and another to hide the truth that is worth seeking in the name of seekers," interjected Tim.

"Part of the problem," Doug continued, "is that the world sees Christians practicing things that are contrary to the word. John the Baptist and Jesus were nonconformists. Can you imagine if John the Baptist and Jesus walked the earth today? What if John the Baptist came up and said, "You brood of vipers." Jesus came into the temple and turned over the tables and caused a ruckus in the synagogue. We don't see that today because we don't want to offend people. The truth in you is going to offend the lie or the darkness in me.

"Ben said a couple of chapters ago that he once was fond of saying the Holy Spirit was a gentleman, and that He wouldn't cause people to change or be inconvenienced in any way. Whoever thought that up has never had an experience with the Holy Spirit. There have been times in my life when the Holy Spirit has just made me look downright foolish. He has also asked me to do things that I just didn't want to do. But I did it with joy because I wanted to please the Father. It wasn't about me; it was about Him. We have to come into a season of understanding, laying foundation, and calling out people's destiny with the understanding that these things are going to offend people. It is going to offend them out of the judgments that the enemy got them to take up and into the truth of what the Father has called them to be. I am going to take that chance of offending someone in order to bring them into their destiny."

Ben added, "Few people today want to take that chance and if they do want to take the chance, they don't have the tools to do what they need to do, nor do they know how to connect with anyone who can help them."

"Like we said, it is pretty natural for you to be influenced by people you hang around with," said Tim. "You start to talk like them. You start to tell the jokes they tell. When Laurie and I had marriage counseling, we were told to hang out with couples on double dates. Afterward, the two of us were to go out for coffee together and talk about what we liked about the couple in the way they interacted with each other. Also, we were to look at what we didn't like about the way they interacted with each other.

"I think we can use the same principle to figure out who we are spiritually predisposed to be in family with. We can connect to those people who will help anchor us in the word and not get swept up in fashion or hunger for worldly success. You can look at someone and the way they interact with other people and you can peek at their spiritual walk. Then you can wonder 'am I made to reflect God in that same way? Or is that not the way that I'm meant to be?'"

Ben stepped in to clarify, "In other words, the seed of your destiny—the way you are going to be in your eternal purpose—is going to be attracted to other people who are mature in Christ in that same way. Joint to joint connections in the body are like magnets—they attract each other. But you have to know how to get your connection points cleaned off so you can connect together."

"Is that what Paul was talking about when he said to come and follow him and imitate him?" asked Doug. "There again, that is why you need foundation in your life. If you don't know the Father's love, His forgiveness, and your identity in Christ, then what are you going to produce? One of the reasons why we need to practice righteousness and know what God has called us to do is that there are people that might be watching us and want to press into their relationship with us and draw from the resources of our experiences.

"It was Paul's goal to bring every man complete into Christ—not to bring him into his teaching or doctrine or ministry. Who we are in Christ and who someone else is in Christ will have some similarities, but it will have some uniqueness also. I have walked with Ben for fifteen or sixteen years now. However, I still don't play a guitar and sing. Ben doesn't ride a horse and rope a cow. But I can call him into his destiny and bring him into the fullness of who he is in Christ because of the Father. That is discipleship. That is making disciples by bringing people into who they are in Christ."

Doug settled back into his chair again and glanced out the window, which looked like it was covered with a black sheet. There was no moon at all that night.

"It is important that we don't present ourselves as vessels of unrighteousness because it not only affects us but it can affect generations beyond us. I don't say that to put pressure on us to perform, just to call forth our destiny. I don't practice righteousness because I am trying to put forth an image. I do it because I behold the Lord, and because I behold the Lord, I see who He is and I am changed."

"In speaking about what we practice, I want to return to this word addiction," said Ben. "Is addiction always demonic or not? If someone feels like they can't overcome an addiction, what are some tools they can use to overcome it? How do we need to understand that for each other and for ourselves?"

"You can try in your flesh time and time again to overcome patterns, but your flesh is weak. However, if you deal with the issue that caused the door to be opened to the enemy and you close that door, then the outward expression or habit is going to take care of itself." Doug leaned forward and looked up and out the window this time, so he could see the stars twinkling through the trees.

"If you take a man who is addicted to some type of pornography, you can almost always trace his addiction back to something that happened in his childhood. Some perversion most likely happened and he made a judgment about who he was because of what happened to him. As a result, he gets stuck in this need to continually satisfy the judgment he made, which results in an addiction. If you show him that he was a victim in his past and it wasn't his fault, that he was a child and the situation was perverted, and help him break the victim mentality off, then he wakes up and realizes that he is not a bad person, he just had a bad thing happen to him. He realizes that the bad thing that happened to him caused him to make a judgment, and then he can deal with that issue. His mind can be renewed in Christ as to who he is and what will fulfill him. The judgment he was believing has been exposed as an unrighteous judgment. He then can begin to believe God's judgments about him that are true and righteous."

"You mentioned the demonic earlier," said Ben. "Some of us grew up with that being common to our talk, and some of us didn't. How does that enter in? Does it enter in every time?"

"I believe if we are to practice righteousness, we need to receive every benefit given from the Father," Doug said with a slight smile. "He wants a people that are completely His, so Christ came to destroy the work of the devil. There are many accounts in Scripture where Jesus ministered to people who were demon possessed. Jesus discerned what spirit was controlling that person. He addressed that spirit and cast it out. So I believe we need to walk in the gift of discernment also. This is just one of the nine gifts that are given to us from the Holy Spirit to love people well. We have been given authority to cast out demons, heal the sick, and even raise the dead.

"I think it is interesting that even though the disciples were so filled with faith in what Jesus said they would do as believers, they came running back to the Lord and said, 'Jesus, *why* couldn't we cast out the demons?' Oh, that the Church today would have that mindset and not be fearful to ask the Father *why*. Are we ready to hear from the Father that we are not prepared? Are we ready to repent from our unbelief and truly receive and walk in full authority as sons? Are we willing to sacrifice through prayer and fasting to see people be set free?

"I also believe," Doug continued, "that if we walk in the Spirit we will crucify our flesh and not give in to the deeds that come from walking in the flesh. For example, I had a man tell me one time that he needed deliverance. I asked him why he needed deliverance. He said he was addicted to sexual things. I got to talking to him and realized that his struggle wasn't demonic. It was just his flesh, and he needed to learn how to crucify his flesh by learning how to appropriate what God has accomplished through Christ."

"You always say that anything brought into the light will not have inappropriate power over a person," Ben said confidently. "That is one of the ways that you deal with the flesh. If you are hiding something and you're not letting people see it and you're not bringing it into the light, then it is just going to rule you. It does not necessarily mean it is demonic."

"To just blame everything on a demon is a cop-out," Doug answered. "On the other hand, to say there are no demonic forces is also a cop-out."

"I like that," said Ben, always looking for the practical steps. "First, bring it into the light. Then let people help you claim that you are in Jesus. It is okay to have people pray for you so that you can break whatever holds are on you."

"That goes back to the heart of the Father and being connected to one another," Doug pointed out. "There was a time in Jesus' journey in which He needed help carrying His burden. When He dropped the cross, someone came and helped Him carry it. The trap of the enemy is to get us to think that we can or should do it on our own. There are times when each one of us needs a brother to come alongside and help us to carry our load. The Lord has designed it that way. He has designed the body in such a way that one part needs the other part.

"As we mentioned early in the book, there is an inheritance in the saints. When I have a relationship with you, there is an inheritance in you that I can tap into. There is also an inheritance in me that you can tap into in our relationship. In God, I don't have to be everything. I have grace for this but I don't have grace for that. Tim has grace for that so let Tim do that. Let him exercise his grace with his gifting and his purpose of what God has called him to do. That releases me from always trying to be 'Mr. Perfect' because most of the time when I feel like that I am in my flesh anyway. It is okay to realize your shortcomings. It is okay for you to realize that you don't have all the answers."

"That reminds me of my friend Kathy," said Ben, winking at the fact he had changed her name for the story. "She was a good leader and a good visionary but she had begun handling everything in the ministry that she was involved in. If you didn't do your job she would do it for you. If people needed something done, she would go and do it. She got into such a practice of trying to do everything and be everything that it was beating her to death. She was just about to lose her way. It was because she was practicing something that was not really coming from a place of rest and being a daughter of the Father. She was acting like a slave.

"After we talked about the roots of the problem, it came out that when she was young, her mother was an alcoholic and was abusive and couldn't do anything. Kathy, as a young girl, decided that she would have to take care of everything. That was a judgment she made in her heart, and she got into that cycle and couldn't stop. I reminded her that that was not who she was, that was a judgment that she had made and the devil didn't have any control over her to make her be that way. Recognizing that has radically changed her. There is such peace over her now that she has released that judgment against herself."

"There is a grace and peace over you when you are in your element," affirmed Doug. "There have been times when I ministered for ten or eleven hours straight and there was a grace and a peace about it. It was not stressful or burdensome to me. It just flowed. Once the grace lifted from me, then I knew I was finished there. I went away rejoicing and excited because God had done something. I think that is key. If there is not a peace or supernatural strength in what you do, then you are doing it in the flesh and the flesh is going to wear you out. You can tell when there is a grace to do something because it is just flowing, even if it is difficult. If the grace is not there, however, it is just a struggle. I have found that if I'm asked to do something but I don't feel the grace there, it's better if I decline. I will mess it up. Apart from grace, the helping presence of God, all I can offer is my flesh and my flesh is really not that good.

"It's true," said Tim. "Laurie and I have sometimes suffered to follow the Lord, but there's always been a peace about it. It's fun to make unusual choices and do things that the world can't understand and to overcome hard situations when God gives you the grace to handle them. I wish I had known earlier how to discern whether God's peace was covering something for me or whether I was striving in my flesh."

"One thing I really stress to my spiritual family is the importance of resting in the Lord," said Ben. "Resting in the Lord is important. Some people use rest as an excuse to be lazy, but resting in the Lord is different. I may be very busy but I am still resting in the Lord because I have grace for what I am doing. If someone asks me to do something, I can turn them down, but there is no condemnation there because I am resting in the Lord. I don't have grace for what they are asking me to do at that time.

"The Bible talks a lot about the Sabbath. Taking some time even one day a week where you not only rest your body, but you do things that re-create you and rejuvenate you. I think the Lord requires one day of that not so that we can destroy ourselves the other six days, but so that He can show us how to work the other six days from a state of rest based on the rest in Christ we have on that one day.

"You can be busy and still be lazy," continued Ben. "If you have no idea who you are and where you are in the Lord, then you can be busy all day and still be lazy because laziness is the refusal to take up your true responsibility. How many of us with children have watched them pretend to be 'busy' so they wouldn't be asked to do something? We need to reconsider our lifestyles and find out who we really are, what God really has for us…and then get to work!"

Doug affirmed, "When we focus on our identity in Christ then it is easy to practice the things Christ would do. It is no longer I; it is Christ that is in me. So I am at rest in Him. We could make things so complicated, but it is so simple. I think the simplicity of the gospel is Christ in you, the hope of glory.

"One thing about being around family and understanding family is this: Think about what you consistently experience when you're around someone. That consistency is what they practice. When the world sees us practicing righteousness, relationship, and rest on a consistent basis, then when we do something silly they realize, 'Hey, there is some common everyday Joe in that guy.' But we know that we are not defined by that silly thing we did and continue on practicing righteousness."

Tim smiled. "It gives others hope that they can be what God has called them to be too, because we are all going to make mistakes, but our mistakes don't jump up and twist our arms until we fall out of Christ where they can defeat us like tiny Christian Kung-fu warriors."

Doug paused to enjoy the colorful word picture, laughed, then continued: "We have freedom to do what God puts in our hearts without worrying about failure because failure doesn't have power over us. We are not bound by the law anymore. In Romans 8 we learn, 'because through Christ Jesus the law of the Spirit of life set me free from the law of sin and death. For what the law was powerless to do in that it was weakened by the sinful nature, God did by sending His own Son in the likeness of sinful man to be a sin offering. And so He condemned sin in sinful man, in order that the righteous requirements of the law might be fully met in us, who do not live according to the sinful nature but according to the Spirit.'

"Where the Spirit of the Lord is, there is freedom. We have freedom to do whatever we want to do. What is cool about that is that we have the nature and character of Christ in us and we are in Him, and so we are not going to violate the things of the law even though we are not under the law, so we don't take our freedom as an excuse to sin. Christ fulfilled the law. Our identity is not in keeping the law. Our identity is walking as sons in the Spirit."

"It is not about changing our behavior. It is about reflecting the new life inside of us with our behavior," said Tim, reinforcing the truth in his own mind.

"It is not what I do, but who I really am," added Ben.

"Yes, and not what you do, but why you do it that shows who you think you are," said Doug. "What are you practicing? What are you presenting yourself to? Let the Holy Spirit give you a revelation about that."

REJOICING IN SUFFERING

The sun rose early and spilled through the mountains, bounced through the aspens and evergreens, and long after it chased the darkness from the sky it made its way into the southern windows of the camper. Inside the men were waking to a cruel reality: the heater had gone out during the night.

"Holy cow, my feet are cold," muttered Ben as he stumbled passed the kitchenette to try and read the thermostat. He had trouble without his reading glasses. "I think it's below 50 degrees in here. Doug, the propane ran out last night."

"Well, now you know how long one tank will last you," Doug announced from the bed in the rear of the RV. Doug was a consummate early riser. All the years of ranching and farming had built into his internal sense of timing the instincts of a farm rooster. Years of living with his wife, Rita, however, had trained him not to make rooster noises when he first awoke, but to lie still, think, and pray until other human beings might be awake as well.

"You said you thought it would go for three nights," Doug said.

"This time we only got two and a half," chuckled Ben. "It ran hard last night because of that cold snap."

As Ben opened the blinds on the window over the small dining nook, he noticed the ice crystals that had formed around the edges of the windows. Looking out over the high country scene, he saw the grasses were covered with frost and glistened in the early light.

"I can still make coffee with the generator and my electric kettle," Ben announced. After putting on several layers of clothing and a knit hat he went outside and fired up the generator, which would no longer start with the simple ignition switch inside the camper. It took some manual nurturing of tiny engine parts and some verbal coaching before it would start, especially on such a cold morning.

When Tim finally arrived from his short drive to the campsite, Doug and Ben had already consumed a pot of french press coffee and had made a sizable fire in the pit. "Hey, Tim, how'd your heater do last night?" asked Doug with a smirk angled towards Ben.

"Well," said Tim, "if you are referring to my furnace, then I would say it was just okay, but if you are talking about my wife's natural bed-warming abilities then I would say I was pretty comfortable."

"Please don't rub it in."

"That's not fair," said Ben, rubbing his hands over the fire. "I don't want to hear anything about your warm bed. I think my toes were blue this morning when I woke up."

The men fired up the generator once more, made one more steaming pot of Joe, and then Ben reached for the small voice recorder. "I don't want to draw any gratuitous connections with our lack of heat last night and our subject for this chat...but aren't we going to talk about suffering?"

Doug picked up on that last cue and began: "In II Corinthians 4:17, it states, 'Our light and momentary troubles are achieving for us an eternal glory that far outweighs them all. So we fix our eyes not on what is seen but what is unseen. For what is seen is temporary but what is unseen is eternal.' If we understand that the momentary light afflictions, sufferings, and adversities we encounter are temporary things that are bringing forth eternal purposes in us, then we understand how to rejoice in our suffering."

"See, Ben, God is just trying to build your character," said Tim.

"It didn't work," responded Ben. "It just made me grumpy."

Doug went on, "Learning to rejoice in suffering is another of the foundational parts of walking with Jesus. There are five points I'd like to make to help bring us into a better relationship with the adversity in our lives. First, *God uses difficult circumstances to develop our character.* The gifts and callings of God are without regard to mens' failings. The gifts He gives us are pure, but what happens is our character and our integrity can't handle what we're entrusted with sometimes, so God has to use circumstances to help develop our character so that we will be Christ-like both in our walk and in our understanding.

"When we find ourselves in the midst of suffering, tribulations or something that we do not really like, we need to understand that God is using that for our good to establish His eternal purpose in us and to bring forth Christ-like character in us. God wants us to be men and women who have substance and the character of Christ in us as we walk in the purposes for which God has called us.

"Jesus says, 'I have told you these things, so that in me you may have peace. In this world you will have trouble. But take heart! I have overcome the world.' It is exciting to me because Jesus tells us that we're going to have problems and that things are going to happen to us, but we don't need to worry because He has given us peace. He has not given us peace that the world gives but His peace passes all understanding. In the world we are going to have tribulation but we need to take heart because Jesus has overcome the world."

"You really can have peace in the midst of trouble," Tim said. "Most people, when they get into trouble the first thing that they lose is their peace. The peace that the world gives is dependent on circumstance and one's understanding of the circumstance. But the peace the Lord gives is beyond understanding, so it doesn't get shaken when a circumstance or your understanding of it changes."

"A lot of people try to pray their troubles away," Ben reflected. "I'm not advertising that we should not pray some troubles away. I'm just saying that our obsession with having a trouble-free life by rebuking all manner of trouble, regardless of discernment, is not the way it should be."

"Sometimes when you rebuke trouble nothing happens because you are actually rebuking God, who has allowed the trouble to happen in order to work for our good," Doug explained. He opened his Bible and read aloud from James 1: "'Consider it pure joy, my brothers, whenever you face trials of many kinds, because you know that the testing of your faith develops perseverance.' And then over in Matthew 5:11 it says,

"Blessed are you when people insult you, persecute you and falsely say all kinds of evil against you because of me.'

"You see, trials and hardships can be a purpose of the Lord in our lives. Hebrews 12 really draws this point out...I am going to read verses 5-11: 'My son, do not regard lightly the discipline of the Lord, nor faint when you are reproved by Him. For those whom the Lord loves He disciplines, and He scourges every son whom He receives. It is for discipline that you endure; God deals with you as with sons; for what son is there whom his father does not discipline? But if you are without discipline, of which all have become partakers, then you are illegitimate children and not sons. Furthermore, we had earthly fathers to discipline us, and we respected them; shall we not much rather be subject to the Father of spirits, and live? For they disciplined us for a short time as seemed best to them, but He disciplines us for our good, so that we may share His holiness. All discipline for the moment seems not to be joyful, but sorrowful; yet to those who have been trained by it, afterwards it yields the peaceful fruit of righteousness.'

We need to understand that in the world we will have trouble, but we take courage because Jesus has overcome the world and has given us His peace. We have to have our identity in Christ because that is where the peace is. We can't have peace that passes understanding in the world in the midst of tribulation and suffering outside of Christ."

"I like how you just read that Scripture and then just moved on," smiled Tim. "I thought you were going to explain it, but you just went on to your next thought. You're right. It doesn't really need explaining; it's quite clear. One thing I'd like to point out, though, is that it plainly says to 'endure hardship as discipline,' not to wait for God to tell you if your hardship is discipline. If

Romans 8:28 tells us, 'All things work together for the good of those who love God and are called according to His purpose,' then I can accept any kind of hardship, or 'trials of many kinds,' as discipline for my ultimate good."

"That's fortunate," said Doug, "because my second point is this: *I've noticed that life is a series of problems. Every time you solve one, another is waiting.*

"Jesus told us that in the world we would have tribulations. I think that God promotes you by the way you handle your problems, endure, and overcome. He who is faithful in little things will be ruler over many. There is a principle that as we become faithful and are able to handle various situations without murmuring, getting mad, cursing God, and kicking the dog on the way out, then we are coming into our ability to rule as sons instead of reacting as orphans. We know that the trial is working character and purpose in us, so God is able to promote us because He knows that He can trust us with more of the administration of His kingdom."

"Does it really matter where the suffering comes from?" asked Ben. "Whether your trouble is a germ from the food you ate or a tribulation that God gave you because you needed a harder row to hoe? Does it really matter where the suffering comes from if it gives the opportunity to rise up and handle it?"

"Usually, the first place my mind goes when I get into any kind of suffering or trouble is that I wonder what I am doing wrong," said Tim.

"That reveals your heart. You just confessed your heart," said Ben with kindness.

"Yep. Probably shouldn't have done that in a book." Tim gave a crooked smile.

"If something happens to me, if I get sick or I find myself in some situation," said Doug, "the first thing I do is ask the Lord what it is about. I ask Him before I rebuke the adversity because if it is an attack of the devil against me then I want to fight the fight of faith and resist the devil. But if it is God dealing with me and working something in me, then I want to submit to the journey and allow it to have its work in me. I figure, the more that I embrace the journey, the quicker it will get worked in me. Sometimes we miss out on what God wants to work in us, so we end up doing it time and time again because we don't have the wisdom to understand that what is working in our lives is for our good."

"I love this line, so I'm stealing it, right here in front of you in your own book," said Tim, turning to Doug. "There are two things I know. One, *God loves me*; and two, *He's killing me*."

Doug smiled in appreciation for the theft of one of his favorite sayings and went on. "From a certain perspective, we wouldn't want to believe a loving God would use tragedies and tribulations to refine us. However, God is no respecter of men. God is willing to require that I die so He can live His life through me. In the analogy of being refined by fire, I guess He has more regard for the treasure He is bringing forth in me than for my expectations of what should or should not burn and how hot the fire should get.

"In I Peter 4 it says, 'Beloved, do not be surprised at the fiery ordeal among you, which comes upon you for your testing, as though some strange thing were happening to you.' Isn't that the first thing you think? 'This is strange.' Then it says, 'but to the degree that you share the sufferings of Christ, keep on rejoicing, so that also at the revelation of His glory you may rejoice with exultation.'

"What happens in trials if you are not secure in God's love for you and you are not secure in your identity in Christ? The devil will tell you that it is not fair because you have not done anything wrong and now you have to endure this. That is the mindset that the devil tries to put on us. He tells us that if God was a loving God He would not be allowing this to happen.

"But think about it. Jesus did nothing wrong—He did everything He saw the Father do and say—yet He learned obedience through the things He suffered. That is an amazing Scripture, Hebrews 5:8. Here the Son of God comes on the earth and does nothing but what was pleasing to the Father but it says, 'even though Jesus was God's Son, He learned obedience from the things He suffered.'

"That is amazing," said Tim, "and if Jesus suffered, why should we think that we should be spared when He said, 'All men will hate you because of me [...] A student is not above his teacher, nor a servant above his master.'"

"True," said Doug. "Everybody likes the first part of Matthew 5. It says, 'Blessed are the poor in spirit, for theirs is the kingdom of heaven. Blessed are those who mourn, for they will be comforted. Blessed are the meek, for they will inherit the earth. Blessed are those who hunger and thirst for righteousness, for they will be filled. Blessed are the merciful, for they will be shown mercy. Blessed are the pure in heart, for they will see God. Blessed are the peacemakers, for they will be called sons of God.' But it's harder to like the rest of the passage. Listen to this: 'Blessed are those who are persecuted because of righteousness, for theirs is the kingdom of heaven. Blessed are you when people insult you, persecute you and falsely say all kinds of evil against you because of me. Rejoice and be glad, because great is your reward in heaven, for in the same way they persecuted the prophets who were before you.'"

Doug looked at Ben and Tim with a half-smile and continued, "When people ask the Lord to bless them they need to know what they are asking. The Scripture says we are blessed when we are persecuted. We are blessed when people speak evil things and have evil thoughts against us."

"I have been praying lately from the Lord's Prayer, 'Your kingdom come,'" said Ben, "but now you tell me the Scripture says 'blessed are those who are persecuted because of righteousness, for theirs is the kingdom of heaven.' I just don't like how those two things go together—*suffering* and the *kingdom coming*."

"What happens when you're out there proclaiming what God is putting in your heart?" Doug asked. "People can be mad at you. They can insult you. The key when that happens is not to react and defend yourself. The key is just to rejoice and be glad that you are worthy to be included in the sufferings of Christ. Most of us, when we encounter persecution, try to defend and justify ourselves. John Moreland, one of my fathers in the faith, made a statement: 'When you are right, you don't need a defense. When you're wrong, you don't have one.' Either way, there's really just no reason to defend yourself. God is our defender. I would rather trust in God's ability to redeem the situation than trust in my own ability, which would mess up the situation. That's why it says that when those things are happening to you to rejoice and be glad. That is tough, and I really don't understand that I have to suffer sometimes to learn things, but that's how it is," admitted Doug.

Tim and Ben agreed.

"It gets even better though," Doug said. "My third observation about rejoicing in suffering is that *sometimes we suffer for someone else.* This one I really don't like. I don't mind suffering for what's going to benefit me. But do I really have to suffer for what is going to benefit you? Why don't you just do your own suffering and just leave me alone?

"In II Corinthians 1:3 it says, 'Praise be to the God and Father of our Lord Jesus Christ, the Father of compassion and the God of all comfort, who comforts us in all our troubles, so that we can comfort those in any trouble with the comfort we ourselves have received from God. For just as the sufferings of Christ flow over into our lives, so also through Christ our comfort overflows.'"

"This is so encouraging," Doug said sincerely. "That God—who is the God of all comfort—knows that in the midst of our suffering we need comfort. He comforts us because He loves us and then we will be able to comfort our brother when he is in the same trial or circumstance. We can comfort him because God has been our comforter. Sometimes God allows us to go through suffering so that when someone else is suffering we can minister confidence to them in the midst of their sorrow. We can tell them of the faithfulness of God that we have experienced."

"That's valuable," said Tim. "When I suffer I do not have the ability to hear much from anyone who has not suffered. His words might be well-intentioned, but they don't have the weight of words from someone who has suffered."

Ben agreed, "This is something we can agree with after the fact, not something that we can agree with in the midst of our suffering, though. In the midst of our suffering we think it's not right, but then later on when we meet a brother who is walking through something similar, we're glad when our words mean more. For example, if you are going through a divorce, words of comfort from someone who has not been divorced are well-intentioned but hard to hear. But someone whose marriage has blown up, who has walked through the same fire, has words that make you feel like someone just put their hand on you. We can be grateful for things in retrospect. While our suffering through hard times is not enjoyable, it is wonderful to think that even those times can be redeemed for someone else's good later on."

Doug agreed, "If you take a man who is in the midst of suffering and who knows he has not done anything wrong, then someone who has already been through that suffering can come up and encourage him that God is just working some eternal purpose in him. 'It will pass quickly,' we can say, 'get your hope in the Lord.'

"A lot of times," he continued, "we need to realize that our suffering brings out friends who are like the friends of Job. When we are in the midst of something, they will come out and say that we must've done something wrong. They will ask, 'What kind of sin did you do? You must've really done something wrong to get God that upset.'"

"Going through suffering," ventured Tim, "keeps us from being so-called Job friends.

Doug added, "I find that when I go through tribulation and suffering, it is good for me to ask the Lord, 'God, I know this is working for my good, so show me the part that is good so I can focus on that and not worry about that other stuff.'"

"If you do something stupid like jump into a briar patch with no clothes on," said Ben, watching Doug and Tim cringe, "then you're going to suffer the natural consequences of a very bad choice. But even when we face more 'mysterious trials,' at least we have some answers that Job did not have. We know that Jesus suffered, yet He lived perfectly and He did not commit any sin. There is no reason in the world, if we know how much the Father truly loves us, for us to let suffering convince us that God is mad at us. We have an answer that Job did not have in the light of being in Christ. If we are clothed in Christ then we know that we are totally righteous in the Father's eyes. He's not punishing us because we did something wrong."

"There is no punishment in perfect love," he proclaimed. "I John 4:18 says that perfect love casts out the fear of punishment.

"So, there may be natural consequences of jumping into a briar batch," he smiled. "If you are just dumb enough to do it, then get ready to suffer some. I guess we could pray for God to turn the thorns into rose petals, but I don't think that is going to be your guarantee. But suffering is not the worst thing. The worst thing is to feel that you have been rejected or pushed away from God because of failure. The worst thing is to feel as though you've been punished by God because you don't measure up. Since we know He doesn't do that, we can really have hope in suffering."

"The principle is that all things work together for my good," said Doug. "I know first of all that God loves me, and secondly I know that He has called me for a purpose that He predestined for me. Then thirdly I know that He is conforming me to His image so that I will be more like Him. Faith is the assurance of something that we hope for, but confidence is something that we have already experienced. When I have been through something and I have seen the hand of God, I don't have to exercise faith that God is going to bring me through it again because I know He will; I have already experienced God's faithfulness in that area.

"A man with an experience—you can't talk him out of it or rob him of it. I know that God heals because He has healed me. The things I know about God are the things that I have experienced with God. They are not something I just heard someone teach about. They are not something that I have seen in someone else. They are things that I have walked through with my own feet. Therefore, I know who God is and how He does it because I have the experience. What I share is not some revelation that I got from some book. I share the experiences that I have had walking with the Lord. That is what brings people into the simplicity of knowing that God is good.

"Paul tell us in Colossians 1, 'Now I rejoice in what was suffered for you, and I fill up in my flesh what is still lacking in regard to Christ's afflictions, for the sake of His body, which is the Church.' How can there be anything lacking in Christ's afflictions? We the Church are the body of Christ, and so as we walk together through trials, it is as though Christ is suffering with us. Aren't you glad when it's all said and done and the dust has settled that someone has been there and has walked through it with you? It is salvation to me."

"If you truly walk with anybody in this life you will suffer for them," stated Ben plainly. "If people you love suffer, then your heart is going to suffer like Christ would suffer for them. He feels for us. He understands our pain. If you are going to walk as Christ walked and live in Him that means you are going to suffer just because you love others like He loves them. He is going to put that love into you. You cannot avoid that kind of suffering."

"When you walk with someone in the midst of a nasty situation, sometimes you find yourself catching all the flack," said Doug. "People will say, 'Why are you hanging around that jerk? What are you doing with him?'

"Then you say, 'Well, number one, I don't see him after the flesh, I see him after the spirit. And number two, God chose and appointed him and he is my brother, my family.' So you choose to bear that suffering and persecution on his behalf because you are his friend."

"When we love like God loves," said Ben, "we don't abandon even those who hurt others or have made mistakes. There is a certain kind of friend who only stays and stands on the stage with you if everybody's applauding and you're having a good time. This is ordinary friendship. However, there are times in your life when you're holding a card in front of you with numbers across it."

"After your arrest?" asked Tim.

Ben nodded a yes.

"That's when the cop says, 'Turn to the left,' and he takes your picture. Then he says, 'Look straight ahead' and he takes your picture. There are only a few guys that will stand beside you when you have that picture taken. That is the friend who is closer than a brother. I think that is the love that God has for us. Jesus is willing to walk with us and not abandon us when we have been arrested for the crimes of our life. If we can get that love in our hearts, too, then we can stand with those around us—but we have to suffer with them because our reputation goes with them."

"You may not agree with what they have done but yet you still walk them through it," said Doug. "Isn't that the ministry of reconciliation? Isn't that the heart of the Father? Sometimes it seems to me that Christians are some of the meanest people on the earth, because they 'kill' their wounded and hurting. They don't want to be associated with people who are wounded or hurt because it might affect their testimony to the community. They think it might make them look bad if they hang out with people who are wounded and hurt. But I believe that is one reason Jesus came to the earth—to save, heal and deliver and to reconcile men back to God."

"This is very practical," said Ben. "One way you could look at it is that the Church is Christ's body. Since the world cannot receive Christ and His kingdom, it follows that His body in this world will continue to receive rejection. Metaphysically speaking, you could say that as His body we're going to continue to receive His afflictions. If you are not receiving rejection it might be that you are in no way exemplifying Christ and His kingdom..."

"Which is precisely what that Scripture that we read earlier says," interrupted Tim, "'If you are not disciplined, then you are illegitimate children and not true sons.'"

Ben looked at Tim, pleased that he had made that connection.

Tim continued, "It is truly favor from God to be allowed to struggle through some things and suffer and have your identity threatened, and ultimately to come into the adoption of sons and the destiny of who you're called to be in Christ, which is wondrous joy. Compare that kind of person to the one who gets everything he wants and always thinks that those external things define him. It is not very fun to be around that person. It is not very fun to be that person. But God knows what we will be."

"That brings me to my fourth point: *Problems force us to look to God and depend on Him, instead of to ourselves. Let me make* this point personal: I have several personal testimonies, so I know this is true. We lived in Texas from 1983 to 1986 and made some bad investments in the oil business. We lost a lot of money and basically were broke. The Father moved us back to Oklahoma and I made the statement that I was a good farmer and I could get back into farming and ranching and get out of debt. I said that I could raise cattle and grow cotton and wheat and everything would be fine in a couple of years. I told this story earlier, but now that I've told you the context, I'll tell you the rest of the details, too.

"So the first year, you'll remember, I planted my wheat crop. But right before we got ready to harvest the wheat, a hailstorm came. It destroyed my wheat. So instead of getting out of debt I went farther into debt.

"I thought, 'that's okay,' because my cotton was growing up and my cattle were looking good. I got ready to sell my cattle, and a week before I was to ship my cattle, my cattle started dropping dead. I called the vet and he said they were healthy looking and he didn't know what was going on. He cut the dead ones open and did some tests and found out they died of lead poisoning. Somebody had thrown a bunch of batteries out in one of the corners of my field. The batteries burst open and the cattle were licking the lead parts and they were dying of lead poisoning.

"I told the Lord that that was okay because I still had a good cotton crop. Right before we got ready to harvest the cotton to sell it, a hail storm came and destroyed my cotton crop.

"You have to realize that through this process I am still ministering the gospel; people are getting saved, baptized in the Holy Spirit, and getting delivered. It is not like I'm living in some big sin. I am still doing the work of the kingdom and the Lord was blessing my labors. But when my cotton was destroyed, I asked the Lord, 'God, what is happening here?'

"What came to my mind was the year before when I had said I was a good farmer and rancher, so I could make it happen. I thought I could get out of debt by my own abilities. God said to me, 'I just wanted to show you what you could do.'

"I asked him, 'Couldn't you have just told me?'

Doug smiled and looked at both Tim and Ben.

"But I know now because of what I experienced. You could have told me that I couldn't get it done, or that I shouldn't trust in my own strength, but I still would have questioned you. When God showed me what I could do, then I understood.

"He gave me Jeremiah 15 where it says, 'Cursed is the one who trusts in man, who depends on flesh for his strength and whose heart turns away from the Lord. He will be like a bush in the wastelands; he will not see prosperity when it comes. He will dwell in the parched places of the desert, in a salt land where no one lives. But blessed is the man who trusts in the Lord, whose confidence is in Him. He will be like a tree planted by the water that sends out its roots by the stream. It does not fear when heat comes; its leaves are always green. It has no worries in a year of drought and never fails to bear fruit.'

"The next season I planted cotton and the boll weevils hit my cotton. A lot of the other farmers were spraying and killing the boll weevils but I wasn't spraying. I went out and picked up one of the boll weevils and I talked to it. People were driving by watching me talk to this boll weevil. And I said, 'Boll weevils, the word says that God rebukes the devourer. You are devouring my cotton crop. I rebuke you in Jesus' name and I appropriate the blood of Jesus over my cotton field and I command you to leave in Jesus' name.' That year I had some of the best cotton in the county. I had made the Lord my trust, instead of trusting in my ability to farm.

"I had some persecution, suffering, and ridicule from my friends. I would have probably done the same thing had I seen Tim out there talking to a boll weevil and commanding it to leave his cotton in Jesus' name. When I did that, my trust was not in my ability to perform; my trust was in God's ability to do what He said He could do."

"Before someone tries to turn your experience into a formula," warned Ben, "we want to remind everyone that God, like any Father, wants His boys to work and be productive. This is not a story about a weird sadistic thing that God does to you in a reality vacuum."

"He was dealing with Doug's prideful trust in his flesh apart from God," noted Tim. "Again, God isn't as concerned with what you do, as He is with why you do it and the state of your heart and relationship with Him."

Ben continued, "Yes, the reason the arm of the flesh doesn't come to anything good is because God wants to be near us and anything we do that starts to put a divide between us and the Father is really coming against the work of Jesus. At this point we remember Ephesians 2 and that Jesus has brought us near to God with His own blood. The nearness is what we enjoy in Jesus and what the Father wants. Whenever we start going off and doing our own thing and think that we can do it alone, everything blows up for us. It is the jealous love of our Father. It is kind of nice to know that His love for us would require us to suffer in order to learn. At least He doesn't leave us alone like some passive, uncaring cosmic parent."

"I see," said Tim. "Isn't that why kids run away? They want to know that it would matter to someone that they're gone." He turned to Doug. "Better to get a hailstorm of discipline followed by some loving words from the Father, than for Him to say 'See ya. Hope that flesh thing works out for you. Try not to let the door hit you on the way out.'"

Doug clarified, "I am not saying that God sent the hailstorms. I am saying that the hailstorms came. I'm saying that in the midst of them I learned a principle that now, twenty some years later, has brought me to a place in which I am able to do things now that I wasn't able to do then because of what God worked within me for good. God used those storms and someone dumping batteries on my land to help me learn to rely on and trust in Him instead of myself."

Doug took a deep breath. "The final point I want to make about suffering and why we can rejoice in it is that *we learn obedience in suffering.*

"We talked about this Scripture a little bit ago. Although Jesus was the Son of God, He learned obedience through the things that He suffered. When Jesus was in the garden, He said, 'Father, if you are willing, take this cup from me; yet not my will, but yours be done.' He told the Lord that He was suffering but yet He chose to ask that not His will but the Father's will be done. He obeyed in the midst of His suffering. So He can relate to us in the midst of our sufferings. I've never had to die. I've never had to shed blood. I've never been whipped. I've never hung on a cross for someone. But Jesus did, and He suffered in obedience so that we could know that He has been there when we suffer, too."

"It is like when Paul was going back to Jerusalem," said Ben. "The prophet, Agabus, came to him and told him that if he went to Jerusalem they were going to bind him in ropes. He even acted it out in a little theater for him so he could make sure that Paul could get a clear picture of what was going to happen. Paul had to look at it and tell him, 'What you see may be the truth, but I have to obey the Father. I am just going to have to go.' He was obedient in his suffering as well."

Doug said, "Then we have Shadrach, Meshach and Abednego, who were thrown into a furnace for not bowing down to a false god. They came out of the fire unhurt, unsinged, and they didn't even smell like smoke when it was over! We all have testimonies where the Lord has asked us to do things and we knew those things would cost something and they would hurt. But when we went ahead and pressed into it, we came out smelling of no smoke. I believe that if we learn how to rejoice in our suffering, we will become the testimony that the Father wants us to be to our generation."

"In my own life," said Tim, "I find that in the midst of my suffering I can do one of two things. I can look at my suffering and say, 'Woe is me.' Or the other thing I can do is look to my Father and say, 'Hallelujah! Thank you for loving me and conforming me to your image. Lord, I know this is working good for me. I don't know what it's working right now but I know there is something.'"

"When I begin to worship the Lord in the midst of my suffering what happens is that God inhabits the praises of His people," said Doug. "I don't know how many times I have found that when I begin in the midst of my pain, sorrow and circumstances to worship the Lord, the peace of God which passes all understanding floods my soul. Then the suffering and persecution that I'm going through seems like a momentary and light affliction, as Paul said. So the reason I choose to rejoice in it is that it brings forth relief and it gets my eyes off the temporal things and onto the eternal things. That is my own life and my own testimony. Is it easy? No! However, as David once said, 'Soul, bless the Lord!' David had to rule his soul. He told his soul, 'Soul, bless the Lord. And all that is within me bless the Lord!' It is a choice."

Tim nodded and said, "We receive a harvest through our perseverance, but if nothing ever happened to test us or question whether our faith was well-placed, then it wouldn't produce anything worth keeping."

"You are talking about Romans 5," said Doug. "It says, 'Therefore, since we have been justified through faith, we have peace with God through our Lord Jesus Christ, through whom we have gained access to by faith into His grace into which we now stand; and we rejoice in the hope of the glory of God. And not only that, we also rejoice in our suffering, because we know the suffering produces perseverance; and perseverance produces character; and character produces hope; and hope does not disappoint us, because God has poured out His love into our hearts by His Holy Spirit whom He has given us.'"

"So perseverance in suffering produces hope," summarized Tim, "and hope does not disappoint because we hope in who God is—the one who pours out love on us through His Spirit!"

Ben closed his notebook where he had been taking notes. "If you didn't know that God loves you then there would be no way that you could create a way to understand suffering. It is not a possibility. You cannot trust God if He is not a God who is love. Otherwise you could take every suffering to court and ask the Lord to prove to you that the suffering is okay. People do this. They take God to court. They take others to court. They take themselves to court over everything related to suffering. It is only the man who has had the love of God revealed to him by the Holy Spirit that can really trust and say, 'It may be hard but God loves me.'"

"Earlier in the passage it says that our faith gives us access to the grace in which we stand," observed Doug. "So God gives us grace for any situation. If we understand this principle then how can we get mad at God? How can we take God to court? How can we curse God and listen to the lie of the enemy or the friends of Job, when we know that God has grace for us in a situation and that He loves us so much that He is bringing us into a place of sonship where He can entrust us with more of what He has for us?

"With all that we have said, it brings new light to this Scripture: 'I consider that our present sufferings are not worth comparing with the glory that will be revealed in us. The creation waits in eager expectation for the sons of God to be revealed.' You can't tell who is a son and who is not without suffering. A man that walks from his intellect can't stand the fire, but the man that walks from his experience comes right through the middle of the fire without smelling of smoke. It reveals him to be a son."

Ben tagged on, "Men who have suffered through the fire and don't come out smelling like smoke are the men that I am more willing to trust and to reveal myself to. If you come to me with intellectual ideas about Jesus and arguments for an intellectual Christianity, and I don't know that you have walked through the fire of suffering, then I get a little nervous."

"That is going back to the principle that you are going to receive comfort from the man who has been comforted by God himself," Doug pointed out. "He doesn't bring you an ideal but the reality of his experience. You can take that to the bank. It is a test of life. In this world we are going to have troubles. I can promise you; you are going to have persecution, tribulation and trouble if you're trying to fulfill your destiny in Christ. On the other hand, I can also promise you that you're going to have the peace of God that passes understanding and the joy of the Holy Ghost moving within you and you are going to be an overcomer. We talked about faith in one of the previous chapters. How can you have overcoming faith if you never have to overcome? How can you have proven faith if you have never had to apply it?"

"We've reviewed a lot of Scriptures in James, Hebrews, and others about how God sees us and loves us in suffering. Are there any other Scriptures that have had a lot of impact for you, Doug, especially in terms of what attitude we can take in the midst of suffering?" asked Tim.

Doug turned a few pages in his Bible to Philippians 3:1 and read, "'Finally, my brothers, rejoice in the Lord! It is no trouble for me to write the same things to you again, and it is a safeguard for you.' Why would rejoicing in the Lord be a safeguard to you in the midst of suffering and trouble? It is because rejoicing gets your mind on the Lord and away from the accusation of the enemy. When we rejoice in the Lord, it takes our eyes off the circumstances and the lies and the accusations that the enemy speaks to us. It puts our minds on the Lord.

"Paul says, as he continues in Philippians 3, "But whatever was to my profit I now consider loss for the sake of Christ." He had been talking about his accomplishments and successes that he'd done in his flesh. He says that he counts those things as nothing for the sake of knowing Christ."

Doug read on, "'What is more, I consider everything a loss compared to the surpassing greatness of knowing Christ Jesus my Lord, for whose sake I have lost all things. I consider them rubbish, that I may gain Christ and be found in Him, not having a righteousness of my own that comes from the law, but that which is through faith in Christ—the righteousness that comes from God and is by faith. I want to know Christ and the power of his resurrection and the fellowship of sharing in His sufferings, becoming like Him in His death, and so, somehow, to attain to the resurrection from the dead.'

"When we die with Christ," Doug explained, "then we are also raised with Christ. Now it is no longer I but Christ in me working through me. So if I understand that principle while praying for someone, it is no longer just me praying for that person, but it is Christ in me that is praying for them. When I encourage someone, it is not just me encouraging them but Christ in me encouraging them. When I comfort someone, it is not just me comforting them but Christ in me comforting them. It is because I count everything else rubbish so that I may find that Christ is complete and adequate in all things.

"Paul goes on and says, 'Not that I have already obtained all this, or have already been made perfect, but I press on to take hold of that for which Christ Jesus took hold of me.' It is my heart's desire that I may lay hold of that in my life which Christ Jesus laid hold of for me, to come into that which Jesus saw in me and God predestined in me to accomplish here on the earth. Everything else is but filthy rags. I believe that when we lay hold of that for which He laid hold of us, His kingdom will be established on earth as it is in heaven.

"He says in verse 13, 'Brothers, I do not consider myself yet to have taken hold of it. But one thing I do: Forgetting what is behind and straining toward what is ahead, I press on toward the goal to win the prize for which God has called me heavenward in Christ Jesus.' What I think Paul is saying here, and what I say, is that I forget about all the failures and all the dumb things that I have done in the past that robbed me from who I was in Christ. I forget about all that because I am under the blood of Jesus and now I am laying hold of and agreeing with that which the Father has said I am in Christ. Suffering will help produce that.

Count it all joy that we may lay hold of that for which Christ Jesus laid hold of us. Now we can embrace suffering, persecution, tribulation and all those things with a new understanding: they are not for my harm but they are for my good."

RULING YOUR SOUL

The three men took some time before lunch to clean up the campsite and tuck the chairs and various pieces of outdoor gear underneath in the RV's storage bays. The uncomfortable morning cold had enhanced the feeling that leaving for home after a few days away was going to be a *good thing*. No one was complaining, but there was a decided air of pack it, clean it, and get it ready to go in all of their movements.

"Look, I have got some leftover pie from the world's biggest store-bought apple pie," Ben said, looking into the refrigerator.

"Warm it up," said Tim.

"No ice cream?" asked Doug.

"Nope. But if we hurry up and finish this book, then I can take you back to where there is some!"

They all agreed it was time to pick up the pace, and so they quickly moved back into their favorite sitting spots.

"In my final chapter I want to talk about *ruling your soul.* The primary Scripture that comes to mind when I think about ruling my soul is I Thessalonians 5:23-24. It says, 'May God Himself, the God of peace, sanctify you through and through. May your whole spirit, soul and body be kept blameless at the coming of our Lord Jesus Christ. The one who calls you is faithful and He will do it.' Also, III John says, 'Beloved, I pray that in all respects you may prosper and be in good health, just as your soul prospers.'

"Well, I have told you already that I'm a selfish person and I want all that God has for me. These passages caught my attention with their talk about prospering and being in good health as my soul prospers. I made the conclusion that my prosperity, my health, and my soul have some kind of connection.

"If my soul is my mind, my will, and my emotions, where does the devil usually attack me first? He seems to always attack my mind first. He always attacks me with a thought that is contrary to what the Lord has said. It is usually a thought that questions the circumstances that I am in.

"In Romans, Paul says, 'Therefore, I urge you, brothers, in view of God's mercy, to offer your bodies as living sacrifices, holy and pleasing to God—this is your spiritual act of worship. Do not conform any longer to the pattern of this world, but be transformed by the renewing of your mind. Then you will be able to test and approve what God's will is—His good, pleasing and perfect will.'

"How am I transformed and set apart from the pattern of this world? Well, like the passage says, it begins with the *renewing of my mind,* so I don't just do what seems normal to my temporal flesh, which is at home in this world. When I'm free from fleshly reflexes, I can discern what the good, pleasing, perfect will of God is. If we let our thinking follow the way of the world, which is temporal, then we produce worldly fruit, and we won't have a clue of what God's eternal plans are.

"You see, the first part of ruling your soul takes place in your mind, learning how to take every thought captive by the word that is hidden in your heart. You learn to take every thought captive by the revelation of what God has spoken to you by His Spirit. If you consider the Scripture in Proverbs that says, 'The mind of man plans his ways but God's purpose is what prevails,' you will realize there has to be a shift in your thinking in order to line up with the purposes of God. It is not a given that your thinking and God's purposes are in harmony. We all have preconceived thoughts of how things should be, but we must allow God to prevail in our thoughts if we want those thoughts to be useful. We have to take thoughts captive and teach them to submit to what the Lord is speaking to us."

"And you are referring to II Corinthians 10:5, which says, 'We demolish arguments and every pretension that sets itself up against the knowledge of God, and we take captive every thought to make it obedient to Christ,' right?" Tim asked.

"Well, yeah. I have a lot more to say about ruling our minds, but I also want to talk about the will and the emotions here. We already talked indirectly about the will in the last chapter. As we said, the best example of ruling your will and making it submit to God is Jesus when He prayed in the garden saying, 'Father, if you are willing, take this cup from me; yet not my will, but yours be done.' Jesus in that moment had a will not to be crucified. However, despite that He knew that His Father could be trusted, and so He submitted His will to the will of His Father. He decided to will what God willed."

"Most of us know that we should not assume that everything we desire or want is from the Lord," said Tim, "but we shouldn't be afraid of our will either. To earnestly desire something for the enjoyment of it is, of course, not a sin. I think it pleases God when we enjoy things, and it's a trick of the devil to make us think that enjoying something is bad unless it's a religious activity. The things we enjoy, and particularly our deep longings and dreams, are usually rooted in the Lord. They are an expression of who He made us to be. God's ideal version of us is not free from desires or dreams or wants. But our flesh can corrupt these things and make us settle for less than what God has for us—something less wild and easier to obtain. A low quality, cardboard version. We need to make sure we're letting the Father speak His good, pleasing, and perfect will to us so we can raise our will to meet His."

Reaching for his notebook, Tim flipped to a bookmarked page and spoke again, "C.S. Lewis said in his sermon, *The Weight of Glory*, 'Indeed, if we consider the unblushing promises of reward and the staggering nature of the rewards promised in the Gospels, it would seem that our Lord finds our desires not too strong, but too weak. We are half-hearted creatures, fooling about with drink and sex and ambition when infinite joy is offered us, like an ignorant child who wants to go on making mud pies in a slum because he cannot imagine what is meant by the offer of a holiday at the sea.' Normally what God dreams for us is better than what we can come up with ourselves. That's why Paul says God's 'good, pleasing, and perfect will.' God made us, so He knows what will be good, pleasing, and perfect for us better than we do. So it's not that we try not to have a will at all, rather, we raise our vision and rule our will to bring it into line with God's heart."

Ben made a full body gesture of agreement.

"We've talked about ruling your mind and ruling your will. Now let's talk about ruling your emotions," said Doug. "Sometimes my emotions are not necessarily the best feelings that I could have. If I am ruled by my emotions, then they would drive me toward wrong actions, and I need to be able to say 'no, I am not going to do that.'"

"What you feel at a given moment may not be of any good value," observed Ben. "In fact, even what you think with your mind when it's devoid of heavy emotion may not have any good value in it, either. You have to stop and ask the Lord what He is saying about your feeling or thought. If you track along with those things without asking the Lord about them, you may find that you went on a trail that may not have anything to do with the Father's heart for you."

"I'll say it again," proclaimed Doug. "God has called us to be *rulers*, not *reactors*. For example," he went on, "if someone comes up and does something that you don't like, your first notion would usually be to pop the guy in the lip. Now, if you take that thought captive and know that it is not a good one to have and it is not the character of Christ, then you can say, 'Brother, I just bless you.' That is learning how to rule in a situation."

"Now, you may actually say any number of things to the guy," said Tim, taking up the imaginary scenario, "depending on how the Lord leads you, but what we're talking about here is a 'being in the drivers' seat' that is befitting sons of God. A sense that you can remain centered in who you are, no matter what the world throws at you.

"A lot of people have never been told that it's good for them to control their own thoughts and emotions. They imagine exercising that control would lead to an unnatural, robotic life of total suppression, but being a ruler and not a reactor is actually a very creative life. Jesus said that if someone hits you on the cheek to turn the other cheek to them as well. Well, that just turns the whole situation on its head. A strike on the cheek is meant to get a certain reaction, but you don't just give the world what it's used to getting when you're a son of God. You become a ruler over the basic principles of the world. As we read in Galations, 'You are no longer a slave, but a son; and since you are a son, God has made you also an heir.'"

Ben chimed in, "That must be what Paul's frame of mind was when he said in Colossians 2:20, 'Since you died with Christ to the basic principles of this world, why, as though you still belonged to it, do you submit to its rules?'"

"We don't walk by what we see or feel," Doug added, "we walk by faith. It is so easy to walk by touchy-feely things and be led astray. Some people build relationships on feelings. If they like what someone is doing, the song someone has sung or the horse someone rode in on, then they feel love and even say 'this is the place I fit.' But on the other hand, if they don't like someone's song or the horse someone rode in on, they say 'this is not where God had placed me.' But it might be precisely where God has placed them, but because they don't feel good there, they're not going to stay. They didn't make their emotion or their thoughts submit to what God may have had to say to them about that.

"In Matthew Jesus says, 'If anyone wishes to come after me, he must deny himself and take up his cross and follow me. For whoever wishes to save his life will lose it.' That word 'life' in the Greek is the same word as 'soul.' So it says, 'whoever wishes to save his soul will lose it but whoever loses his soul, for my sake, will find it.' When I try to maintain my rights and what I want, I can be sure I'll lose them. But if I go ahead and lose what I think

I have and take up what Christ wants me to have then I am going to obtain the fullness of what God has called me to be.

"The passage goes on to say, 'For what will it profit a man, if he gains the whole world, yet forfeits his soul? Or what will a man give in exchange for his soul?' So many times we settle for less than what God has for us because of what turned our emotions on. That's what we think we deserve."

"The person that makes this very practical for me is my wife," said Ben. "Robin is so much more aware of taking thoughts captive than anyone I walk with. I am jealous of her ability to not claim every thought as originating in God or from her own heart. She recognizes that her mind is a place of warfare and that she cannot act on the first thoughts or feelings she has. She is just really aware that there is stuff floating around in the atmosphere, and she wants to tell her mind what it can and cannot do in order to set the rules of the game for the day. I'm always really inspired by that...I want to be like her. I don't want anything setting the rules of the game for me.

"My old foolish nature is to hang on the surfboard of life and surf whatever feelings or thoughts I have right up onto the beach. For those of us who are walking in Christ, however, we really don't want to live by our feelings and emotions but by what the Father speaks to us."

"There is a really good bumper sticker that agrees with that," said Tim. "It says: 'Don't believe everything you think.'"

"Some thoughts come in and we realize that those are not the Lord and that they are not ourselves, either. So we have to be able to discern between the spirits. We actually have dominion over our thoughts and we can decide which ones we keep and which ones we send back," said Doug. "The Scripture says, 'Let this mind be in you which was also in Christ Jesus.' It also says, 'we have the mind of Christ.' In other words, we need the mind of Christ in order to be able to rule those things. And we get the mind of Christ, as we discussed in an earlier chapter, by being in Christ and hiding the word of Christ in our hearts.

"It is so exciting to me because it is the Father's good pleasure to give us the things of His kingdom. It is so important to rule our soul and not to worry about what we need to eat or drink. If we don't rule our soul, then we worry and we doubt the faithfulness of the Father. The Scripture says not to worry about what we'll eat or drink or wear, and Jesus says, 'our Father knows that you need [these things]. But seek His kingdom, and these things will be given to you as well. Do not be afraid, little flock, for your Father has been pleased to give you the kingdom.'"

"Do not be afraid," observed Tim, "is a scriptural command to rule our souls here, and we see it all over the place."

"If you don't know how to rule your soul in a time of anxiousness or want or need then all of a sudden instead of trusting in the Father, you start trusting in things of the world, trying to make things happen in your own strength. As we mentioned in the last chapter, we are to rest in the peace that passes understanding that Christ has given us," said Doug.

"We have to process so many thoughts in one day," added Ben. "Anything that causes us to question whether God loves us might put us on track to fend for ourselves and to try to live in our own strength. These thoughts ought to be taken captive and dealt with early, but it takes a sharp, fast discipline and a real commitment to do that."

"This point can be confusing for some," said Tim. "It has been for me, and so I want to chime in here to answer the people who might read that and say, 'So am I just supposed to sit here and do nothing? I don't know how to rule every thought so can I do anything at all without fear of failing?'" Tim answered his own question as he went on: "We have to remember that we're dealing with two natures here—the old and dead sin nature, and the redeemed and restored life that is in Christ. So when it comes to measuring the amount of work we can do in taking care of ourselves, it's not so much a question of how much effort we expend personally, but where that effort comes from.

"To illustrate, if my effort comes from a lack of trust in the Father to be able to give me what I need or if it comes from a sense that He doesn't care about me, then I've got an issue to deal with because that's not my true nature and the dead man is awake and has managed to take the wheel. However, if my personal effort comes from a place of trust and participation in what God is doing and what He has spoken for me, then *great!* Sometimes He might ask me not to do much and to trust Him with the details. Sometimes He might ask me to do difficult things for a long time, but I can do it in His strength. So again we see—God doesn't so much care what you do, but why you do it."

Tim smiled in appreciation of both his question and his answer as he summarized, "I think the encouragement for myself here is not to sweat the details, but to simply focus on trusting in God and learning to discern when I am striving apart from Him."

"I've been walking with the Lord for twenty-five years," said Ben. "I still feel dumb for thinking dumb thoughts. I wish getting smarter over time would kill all the dumb thoughts, but it hasn't for me. We get so many thoughts or ideas from things we see on TV, something we hear someone say, and a million other small voices we hear every day. I don't think the opportunity to agree with a dumb thought may ever disappear in our journey in this world because we are surrounded by these influences all the time. Maybe I am just learning not to agree with everything I think."

"If the cartoon character of the devil was true and every time he came to us, we could see his red horns and a pitchfork, then we would know that it was the devil. Trouble is, he doesn't come that way. He comes subtly to deceive us," warned Doug. "The only thing the devil can really do to us is to try to convince us into believing a lie. All power and authority has been taken from him. He tries to deceive us into believing the lie that he is the one who has hope for us. That is the only weapon that he has. He deceives us into thinking that God does not love us. He deceives us into thinking that we are not good enough. He deceives us into thinking that no one else struggles with these same things. He deceives us into thinking that we will never obtain anything. And we buy into all of that deception and the end of his deception is death."

"I think that the older and more mature you get the more subtle the devil gets," said Ben. "He will come in and say you need to do something because it is a good thing. He will say that you should go this way because it is a great idea. We really do need to take every thought, every idea, and every grand vision or dream captive for a moment, even if they seem like good, Godly, righteous things at first glance. Then we need ask the Father if those things are what He is talking to us about or if they are something that has nothing to do with His will for us right now."

"Jesus passed up a lot of 'good' things in favor of doing what the Father was doing and speaking only what the Father was speaking," Tim added.

"I think until we are actually dead and buried in the grave, that dumb spirit is always there to feed us some thoughts," said Doug. "I don't really have to look for it. It comes to find me. I think that is why it's so important to understand the foundation of ruling your mind and having thoughts on things above and not on things of this earth. The Scripture says in Colossians 3, "Keep seeking the things above, where Christ is, seated at the right hand of God. Set your mind on the things above, not on the things that are on earth. For you have died and your life is hidden with Christ in God.' We are seated with Christ in heavenly places. We have been set in a place where we are above all rule and dominion."

"Being in Christ means being ourselves," added Ben. "Being ourselves means we are seated with Christ. We have a heavenly perspective. We have an opportunity to hear the Father on everything and He is not going to leave us alone. There's this constant, wonderful opportunity to know who you are, to be at total rest in who you are in Christ, and to make decisions appropriately.

"We could just try and surf every thought and even believe that every *opportunity* comes from the Lord. But how terribly immature that would be. One of my pet peeves is when people think that everything that comes from the Lord comes in the form of an opportunity. I don't want to strike them in the forehead because that would not be helpful, but do I want to encourage them that opportunity is not always synonymous with the will of God."

"I tell people that getting an invitation does not necessarily mean you have to grace to go," said Doug.

"I agree," said Tim. "Open doors are a way God speaks, for sure. Like Doug was saying before, there's a flow when you're in your grace. But doesn't God sometimes ask us occasionally to knock on locked doors and to pass by open ones? The need does not necessitate the call," said Tim. "There are so many needs in the world but that doesn't mean that you need to take care of them all. Sometimes we see an opportunity and think it looks good, so the devil will tell us, 'That looks good. You're supposed to be this Jesus-guy. You should go do that.' Pretty soon we're trying to work to be somebody and we're letting the devil be our judge instead of hearing what the Lord's will is. Maybe the Lord has someone else doing the intercession and He has us going to enjoy the football game. If our identity is in Christ, that should be just fine."

"Just because you see a need does not mean it is the will of the Father for you to address it," said Ben. "If you served every need that you saw, you would be dead in a week."

"Let's look at the life of Jesus," said Doug. "Like Tim said, how many times is it recorded in Scripture that it was Jesus' intent to walk by a situation? I think what you two are talking about is a trap of the enemy. Because we think it's a good work, we feel like we need to do it. Jesus did not give Himself to every good work. He just gave Himself to what He heard the Father say and to what He saw the Father do. We can get distracted by doing good works and then never accomplish what God has given us grace to do."

"We don't live by performance," reminded Ben. "So many believers put things into performance formats and say 'this is what ought to happen.' Then they get into the 'ought to' and 'should do' mode. But our ability to listen to the Father and walk as His sons is *above performance*. When Jesus was at the pools of Bethesda, He just healed one guy, although there were many lame, crippled and sick people there. I imagine Jesus stepping over people who were sick in order to get this one guy. I wonder if the devil came and told Him that He ought to heal all those people."

"In the story of the woman with the issue in her blood," said Doug, "Jesus was on His way to pray for someone else, when He was touched by the woman and felt power go out of Him as He walked by. Jesus knew that the woman was calling out with her need and when she touched Him her need was met. His intention, though, was to just walk on by. He didn't even see her until after she touched Him. And so the trap of the devil in our thoughts is this: 'You really need to go over there because those people really need Jesus. You need to do that because it would be a really good thing.' We can do a lot of good works, but those works are not necessarily what God has given us grace to do."

"*Busyness* does not equal obeying the Lord," said Ben. "Being busy all the time and working hard does not equate with living the life of joy in Christ. It is not the same. Christ might call you to be busy for a season, but He might also ask you to be still and do nothing for a season as well. Neither busyness nor rest are proof that we are obeying the Lord."

"I like how you said that," said Tim. "Being in Christ and walking in Christ is easy for the soul, in work and in rest. I move out of a place of rest, not a place of obligation. I am to move out of a relational leading from the Father about specific things, places, or people that I am to engage. As I go about those things, how could the goodness, love, rest, ease, wholeness, and healing that I experience not fall on a few extras along the way?"

Doug affirmed this beautiful picture as he recounted: "It is recorded in Scripture that as the disciples' shadow fell across people as they walked by, the people were healed. People were set free not because the disciples laid hands on them, but because the power of the Holy Spirit radiated from them as they walked by. I have had that happen. I have been in meetings where I walked down the aisle to go pray for someone and another person got healed just as I walked by. I can't heal anybody, but it is Christ in me and the anointing of the Lord that just saturates people.

"With it being the case that what is in us affects those around us, it's important to be mindful of this next Scripture. It says in I Peter, 'Dear friends, I urge you, as aliens and strangers in the world, to abstain from sinful desires, which war against your soul. Live such good lives among the pagans that, though they accuse you of doing wrong, they may see your good deeds and glorify God on the day He visits us.' One of the important reasons why we need to rule our souls and walk in the manner of Christ is that there are people watching and observing us. We need to be careful how we act because in the day of their visitation, we don't want to be a stumbling block."

"We are in Christ and we are a new creation," said Ben. He paused for effect and then said, "That doesn't imply that we automatically have sense enough to rule our souls. We can walk around dumb as a sack of hammers until the day we die and God will still love us completely, but unless we rule our souls, we will continue to suffer many needless problems. The whole family of God around us can suffer all kinds of things on our behalf if we're not ruling our souls."

"Also if you don't rule your soul then no one will be able to understand what God has done in you in your journey," noted Doug. "It won't be winsome and attractive if you don't take your thoughts captive. Though not ruling your soul doesn't deny the fact that God loves you or that you are totally His, ruling your soul is the discipline of the son who learns to walk according to the Father's word and heart for him all the time. But the son also knows he'd still be a son even if he didn't."

"You cannot agree with everything you feel and everything you think and want. You have to make sure what you think and feel is in agreement with who you really are," said Tim.

"As we've said, to rule our soul is to place each thought, want, or emotion in obedience to Christ," stated Ben. "So you take the thought and ask the Lord what He is doing in it. You say, 'Jesus, what do you say about this at this moment? I want to obey you, Lord.'"

"Now we talked about this next point earlier in the book, but I want to bring it up again because it is so essential to ruling our souls," said Doug. "Hebrews 13:17 says, 'Obey your leaders and submit to their authority. They keep watch over you as men who must give an account. Obey them so that their work will be a joy, not a burden, for that would be of no advantage to you.' This refers not to people who are lording over your faith, but to people who are watching over your soul." The distinction between trying to manage someone's life and the nurturing care of a pastoring heart was one Tim and Ben had heard Doug make many times before.

"A lot of times we get deceived in our soul. That is why God puts people in our lives to watch out for us and to encourage us. They can tell us if our soul is all out of whack. They help us get healthy."

"That is the role of a pastor," affirmed Ben, "someone who has grace for you and loves you. Someone who shepherds and loves people with a heart to build up. Pastoring is not the business of being over a fellowship's administration. It is the business of speaking to people's hearts, one at a time, and reminding them of who they really are."

"That is why I think it's very important that everyone have someone to look to for accountability," proclaimed Doug. "Why does the devil not want us to have accountability in our lives? Because it makes it easy for him to attack our mind, will, and emotions to get us to stray from the truth.

"Being pastored means having someone who wants to see you grow to be complete in Christ," Ben reflected.

Doug affirmed, "Yes, that's the heart of the Father. Everything He did, does, and is doing is to bring us into Him."

"So, we might need help ruling our soul from folks that have the Father's heart," said Ben.

"I need help ruling my soul," admitted Tim.

"It is not something we can do just by Bible study, praying more, and trying harder," explained Ben. "We all need help and it is okay to say that we need help. It is okay for us to say to someone, 'I need help ruling these thoughts about this thing in my journey.'"

"There have been times when I have been strong in one area and weak in another area," said Doug. "If I can find someone who has overcome in the place that I'm weak, I can ask them to help me get victory in that area. I have seen time and time again that what seems to be unsalvageable can come into reconciliation and be restored—to be better than what it was."

Doug took a drink of water, thought for a minute, and then spoke again, "When a kingdom man speaks of ruling, he really only has authority to establish what the king has already put in place. So when we speak of ruling our souls, we are only establishing the fact that the Father has redeemed our souls, or brought them back, from death. Ben, I think you sing a song about that redemption from the pit of emptiness. The Father is the only one that has the original blueprint of how my soul was created to look. And I think it says in Genesis 2 that He created a living soul. So when we feel the pull of death on our souls, we just have to trust, like the psalmist says, that He will restore it, for that is one of the things that the blood of Christ has purchased for us —a redeemed soul. And that is truly a firm foundation for us to stand on. We can say along with the psalmist, 'Return unto your rest, oh my soul, for the Lord has dealt bountifully with you.' We can say, 'Bless the Lord, oh my soul,' for that is truly what we were made for.

"As we begin to trust the Father in the restoration of our souls, we will begin to feel the freedom that the psalmist talked about when he said, 'My soul has escaped, as a bird out of the snare of the fowler.' What freedom! And we can trust that He who began this good work is faithful to complete it. The invitation to 'come unto me, all who are weary [...] you will find rest for your souls' can be an anchor for us—a sure foundation."

Doug paused briefly and then continued. "Several years ago I was driving down the highway and the Lord spoke to me. He asked me, 'Are you convinced that I am able to bring to pass what I have spoken? Are you convinced that I'm able to keep what you have entrusted to me?'

"It got me thinking: what are some of the sure foundations that I really am convinced of in my life? I sat down and made a list one day. What I discovered is that the first thing I am convinced of is that God loves me. I've seen God love me time and time again. I'm convinced that He does. It is the same with these twelve things, which ended up as my list."

Doug turned over a page in his notes and began to read the list, occasionally looking up and embellishing with commentary:

"God loves me.

"God chose me, called me, and He appointed me.

"God will never leave me nor forsake me.

"God is greater in me than the devil is in the world that is opposing me.

"God's word concerning me will not return to Him without accomplishing what He sent it to do for me because God is not going to dishonor and discredit His name by not keeping His word. He's not going to violate Himself.

"God is a rewarder of those that seek Him. God takes pleasure in rewarding faith. God gives us faith because faith pleases Him and then He rewards us for walking in that which He has given us. What pleases God? It is faith. Then as we exercise that faith, He rewards us for it.

"All things work together for my good. There has not been anything that I have encountered in the last thirty-five years that has not worked for my good. That's seven.

"No weapon formed against me will prosper. Why is that? God is for me, so who can be against me? I believe that no matter what people try to do against me, God is my Redeemer and He is the one that will war on my behalf.

"Whatever I ask according to His will, He hears. He will give me that which I ask for.

"The tenth thing that I believe in and am convinced of is that signs and wonders follow me. Why? The Lord says signs and wonders follow those who believe. I don't follow after signs and wonders. Signs and wonders follow after me. So I believe that when I pray for people, things are going to happen. I believe that when I prophesy to people, things are going to happen. I don't seek after the one who ministers healing; I seek after the one who is the Healer."

Tim and Ben frantically wrote in their journals as Doug explained: "In 1974 I went to Kathryn Kuhlman meeting. She was a one-of-a-kind type of gal and she was cool. I'm sitting in this meeting waiting for it to start. This person came up and said, 'God said that if you would pray for me, He would heal me.' I thought 'this is different.' I was a new believer. So I prayed and said, 'Father, heal this person.' Well, they got healed. I thought, 'Man, this is cool.' This was before the meeting even started.

"Then another person came up and said, 'The Father said if you would pray for me He would heal me.' I had just seen this other person get healed and I thought, "Sure." I had more faith now. I said, 'Father, thank you for healing this person.' Then they got healed.

"I sat there having a great time before the Lord. Then the Lord spoke to me. He said, 'See the man in the wheelchair?' I told the Lord I did. The Lord told me He wanted to heal him and that I needed to go pray for him. Now, notice what God did for me. He didn't tell me about the man in the wheelchair first. He let the other two come to me and get healed. Then he showed me the man in the wheelchair. I stepped out and went and prayed for this guy. He got healed, walks out, and leaves the meeting pushing his wheelchair, all before Kathryn ever came on stage. God taught me through the deal that He is never going to require something of me before I am fully equipped and believing He is able to do it.

"If God had told me about the man in the wheelchair first, my response would have been 'Father, Kathryn will be out in a little bit and this is her meeting.' So many times we think we have to chase after someone who is moving in a certain anointing. Many people want to run to a prophet's meeting so they can get prophesied over. They go to find someone who moves in healing so they can be healed, and that is fine.

"But there have been times in my life where I have had to look in the mirror and prophesy to myself. I have had to lay hands on myself and pray for my own healing. If I don't have confidence that God is able to do it for me, then how can I have confidence that God is able to do it for you?"

"You just pointed to both ends of the spectrum of trusting in God for miracles and healing," said Ben. "Somewhere in the middle there's a lot of room. I wish it would become perfectly fine for all of us to allow the family of faith to pray for us, love on us, believe God for what He is doing in us, and expect to see the power of God displayed."

Doug went on with an avalanche of encouragement: "The word says that if you are sick then call the elders and have them anoint you with oil. It also says lay hands on the sick, and they will recover. But there is not just a single pattern in the Bible.

"If you look at Jesus, one time He says 'your faith has made you whole' and someone was healed. Another time, Jesus told someone he had to do this, this, and that before he was healed. Another time, he spit in dirt and put the dirt on someone's eyes and that person was healed. No one knew how Jesus was going to heal. However, people left His presence healed. You cannot just create a formula. You just don't know how He's going to do it. He is God. He just does as He pleases. It says in Isaiah, "I am God, and there is none like me [...] I will do all that I please." He has that right because He is God.

"Where was I?" asked Doug, rifling through his notes for a place in his teaching outline.

"I think that was all part of number ten," said Tim, smiling.

"Okay then, the eleventh thing I am convinced of is that the blessings of the Lord will overtake me.

"Finally, the twelfth and most important thing I am convinced of is that God is able to finish in me what He has begun. God doesn't begin something just to begin it. He always begins something to finish it. He knows the end before He begins.

"I would encourage you to sit down after reading all of this and just pray. Ask the Lord, 'God, what am I convinced about?' When you start writing these things down it settles some issues. Faith comes by hearing and hearing by the word of the Lord. You hear yourself speaking the things that you are convinced of because you have seen God faithful. When the enemy comes in and tells you that God can't, then you can say, 'Ha, ha, ha on you devil. Just stand and watch because I know what I know."

Ben, looking at the list of Scriptures Doug had in his notes said, "It might be a good idea to write out the Scriptures longhand, too. There's something about taking a pen and writing each word, saying each one out loud, that will really help you. Add Doug's list to the things you write down on your own, and you have a good starter kit to help you do warfare against stupid thoughts."

"That's good, Ben," said Doug. "Here are the Scriptures for each of the things I am convinced about.

God loves me – John 3:16

God chose me – John 15:16

God will never leave me nor forsake me – Deuteronomy 31:6

Greater is He that is within me – I John 4:4

His word will not return without accomplishing what He sent it for – Isaiah 55:11

He is a rewarder of those that seek Him – Hebrews 11:6

That all things work together for my good – Romans 8:28

No weapon formed against me will prosper – Isaiah 54:17

Whatever I ask according to His will, He hears – I
John 5:14-15

Signs and wonders follow me – Mark 16:17

The blessings of the Lord will overtake me –
Deuteronomy 28:2

He is able to finish what He has begun – II Timothy
1:12

Ben was excited now. "Readers," he said directly into the
recording device, "tell the Father that you believe these things
even if you just barely do. Stir that faith up. Put your list
somewhere where you will see it every day for a week or two.
Read it out loud and tell the Father that you believe it every day.
This is not about voodoo or spells. This is about speaking the
truth so much that it starts to go into your own ears. It resonates
and agrees with the Holy Spirit in you. When it goes in you then
it starts to take root. Then when the devil comes to give you some
stupid idea, you can take that idea captive immediately because
you recognize that it is not, or that it goes against, what you
believe. You can shoot that stuff down with the Scriptures and
that is really where you can begin to rule and reign in your soul."

"That's hiding the word of God in your heart," said Doug.
"You filter everything and every thought through the word in
your heart—that which is true and that which God has spoken."

Doug folded up his list and put it in his pocket as Ben
reflected, "I became closely acquainted with the concept of
foundation laying years ago when, for the first time, I had to
oversee the building of my house. About six months into the
building process—after the roof was up, the walls were up, and
the windows were in—the floors started sagging in the middle of
the house. My builder had overlooked the most important thing
in the house: the foundation.

"That...is *not* a good thing," quipped Tim.

"Nope, not good."

"I thought, 'If my builder had just taken the time to do the right thing and to put in the right foundation this wouldn't be happening. Nothing else can go on now because the foundation is not right.' I could have been as inventive as I wanted to be on the second or third floor, but unless I paid attention to the foundation, everything else I tried to build would begin to sag and become weak. Obviously, this situation made me very nervous. I thought the whole thing was going to collapse if I didn't take care of it right away, and I had an engineer tell me that very thing.

"I realize that I am starting to wax, but I want to make it very clear: *this is a book about foundations,*" Ben said as he looked at the mini recorder as though it was a microphone to the world and continued. "This is not a book of options. If we can't get these into our hearts right now—pressed down deep at a foundational level—then everything is going to sag and get weak.

"This book has been about foundational things, not optional trim items like paint and shingles. When we get these eight foundations down deep in our souls we can be sure that we will grow mature and strong. We can also begin to trust one another to be as wild and creative as we like in the optional stuff.

"I would encourage every reader to start with receiving the truth of the first chapter, *God's Love,* and then to keep laying foundational truth from there. Submit to these things and put them under your feet and under your future. Put them into your children. Encourage your spouse with them. May God bless every one of these foundational truths in you."

"It's good to know that our Father has set in place good things for us," Doug added. "As Jeremiah tells us, God knows the plans He has for us, and they are real good."

The three guys looked at each other.

"Well, alright," they agreed, nodding as if to show that everything had been said.

◄◄◄

"We'll see what you do with this thing, Lord," said Doug about the whole idea of writing a book. He opened the RV door and stepped outside for some fresh air. "Okay, so you guys are going to go fishing, and I'll stay here until 2:00. If you don't come up the hill with the boat on your shoulders by then, I'll drive the mile and a half to the dam and pick you up there?"

Ben grinned, "I don't know which one will be harder, but I would put money on the second option."

He hesitated a moment.

Tim got his rain gear and fishing rod, and his man-spirit fired up. He knew there was some work ahead, one way or another. Ben packed up the camp stove and the tables, gathered up the trash, and stowed them in their places under the RV. When everything was in order for the ride home, Doug shook Ben's hand and then Tim's, and the fishermen disappeared into the woods.

Tim gazed into the water as he and Ben paddled away from the shore. The blue got deeper and darker, and as any sense that the reservoir even had a bottom became fleeting, he decided looking forward would serve him better. Ben pointed at the huge boulders that jutted up from the water on the far shore and across the long and skinny reservoir's narrower axis.

"Let's try over there," said Ben, unaware that Tim had never paddled into such deep water before or so far from shore.

"Okay" said Tim, who started paddling first as a signal of courage. A few wispy clouds floated by in the upper reaches of the otherwise blue sky. Ben and Tim paused to strip off their outer layers, well-warmed by their efforts, despite the steady, cool breeze blowing up the lake from over the dam.

Arriving at the other shore after paddling across the wind for about fifteen minutes, they stopped and cast some lures toward the structure of the boulders and some fallen trees, reasoning that the fish would be hiding there midday.

There was no one on that side of the reservoir at all. They drifted into an inlet, their lures being tailed, but not taken, by large wise trout in clear blue water. Ben looked at the quaking aspen trees where finches mingled their songs with the calls of seagulls high overhead. He felt a little spray of water the wind blew off the oar and on to his cheek, and thought about how he was floating through what must have once been the sky of a rough, dry, deep canyon before men built a dam and flooded it with water diverted from the Arkansas River.

Looking at his watch, Ben asked Tim, "would you rather paddle back across the narrow part and walk the boat up the hill? Or paddle upwind...oh, I'd say...about five times the length we just paddled across the middle of the reservoir to the dam?"

"Well, it's long, but at least it's flat. Let's go for the dam," answered Tim as the wind tried to blow his hat off.

Ben and Tim pointed the boat across the middle of the huge body of water and started paddling. Soon the wind was right in their faces, whipping them and drawing tears from the corners of their eyes. There was no rain or clouds, just a stiff wind that wanted to blow them back to the upper corner of the reservoir.

Gentle swells turned rougher, cresting white on top, and Ben and Tim positioned the bow of the boat to slice through them. "Glad we're not taking those sideways!" yelled Tim. Out in the dead middle of the reservoir they were tiny, and everything around them seemed to be either bobbing, turning, or swaying in the wind and waves.

"We'll make for that point over there," yelled Ben, pointing to a distant sandbar on the same side of the lake but about halfway to the dam. It looked far to be sure, and Tim thought about how walking the boat up a hill seemed like an easy proposition now.

Tim remembered what he had learned from the dozen or so times he tried whitewater kayaking: 'Paddle forward. The easiest ways to end up underwater are to hesitate, paddle backward, and to be unsure of where you're going.'

Never looking again toward the upper end of the lake, the slope they could have walked, or the direction of camp, Tim dug in and started making powerful strokes toward the point. The boat stabilized as Ben adjusted his paddling in rhythm with Tim.

The two reached the sandbar tired but in good time. They paddled the boat out of the wind in the cover of the high bank which rose into a pine-covered ridge. Warmth and calm returned to their bodies and souls. They spent a few minutes resting and gently paddling to explore the cove, taking the time to cast a few lures near a tree that had fallen in the water.

"It is amazing what wind and a large body of water can turn into," Ben said as he adjusted his cap and got ready to paddle back out into the wind and waves.

Tim and Ben maneuvered the canoe around the point and were hit in the face by more big waves and unforgiving gusts. It had to be done to make it to their landing area near the dam.

They squinted and paddled to the next wind-protected point where they found cover again, at least for a few moments. Then the next. Finally, they paddled up to the picnic area, just upstream from the dam, where they hoisted the boat onto their shoulders and carried it to the truck where Doug was waiting.

"Was starting to wonder about y'all," he said with a grin. "Looked pretty exciting out there. How'd you handle it?"

"Paddled forward," said Tim.

www.timewithdoug.com
www.benpasley.com
www.timfthornton.com

CPSIA information can be obtained at www.ICGtesting.com
Printed in the USA
BVOW010856211111

276451BV00001B/5/P